How to
Recover
from
Grief

How to
Recover
from
Grief

Richard Lewis Detrich
Nicola J. Steele

Judson Press® Valley Forge

HOW TO RECOVER FROM GRIEF

Unless otherwise indicated, the Scripture quotations in this publication are from the Revised Standard Version of the Bible copyrighted 1946, 1952 © 1971, 1973 by the Division of Christian Education of the National Council of the Churches of Christ in the U.S.A., and used by permission.

Other quotations of the Bible are from

HOLY BIBLE New International Version, copyright © 1978, New York International Bible Society. Used by permission.

Today's English Version, the *Good News Bible*—Old Testament: Copyright © American Bible Society, 1976; New Testament: Copyright © American Bible Society 1966, 1971, 1976. Used by permission.

The Living Bible. Tyndale House Publishers, Wheaton, Ill. Used by permission.

Library of Congress Cataloging in Publication Data
Detrich, Richard Lewis.
　　How to recover from grief.
　　Includes bibliographical references.
　　　1. Grief.　　2. Consolation.　　I. Steele, Nicola Jeanne.
II. Title.
BJ1487.D47　1983　　248.8'6　　82-17978
ISBN 0-8170-0989-2

The name JUDSON PRESS is registered as a trademark in the U.S. Patent Office. Printed in the U.S.A. ⊕

This book is lovingly dedicated
to the life, ministry, and memory
of Harland Steele,
father, friend, and co-laborer.

Contents

Preface

Your loved one has died.

Your whole world has turned upside down. Nothing makes any sense any more. You feel very alone and confused. You don't understand what's happening to you. You feel as if your feelings and emotions are out of control. You wonder at times if you are losing your mind.

Not only do you suffer the pain of your loss, but you suffer the additional pain of not understanding this maelstrom of emotional confusion in which you've been caught.

This book is for you! It doesn't have all the answers, but it will help you sort out some of the questions. It will help you to understand better what's happening in your life. And, at some point, it will help you begin to work out a plan for your future.

We're writing this book as a husband-and-wife team. Don't let the difference in names confuse you. When we married, Nikki kept her own name for her own reasons. Dick didn't mind, and our children, well, their name is Detrich—it's Nikki's thing, not theirs.

This book really began when we were asked to develop a "Beyond Sorrow" seminar that would help those who'd lost loved ones understand what they were going through and be able to recover from their grief. Our interest in grief recovery grew, and eventually Dick wrote his Ph.D. dissertation on this subject. In the seminars we sensed a real need for this kind of book.

In this book we want to do the following:

1. Provide you with some information about the grief process through which you are passing. We feel that if you understand what's happening it will be less fearful and you'll be better able to go through your grief.

2. Provide you with some support as you go through this process. We want to assure you that it's OK to grieve. To encourage you to

take your time. (This is a long process!) To encourage you to share your feelings. To assure you that what you're going through is probably perfectly normal for someone who is grieving.

3. Provide a catalyst for your growth. We believe that it is possible for you to take a negative experience like grief and not only *go* through it but also *grow* through it. It's not easy; in fact, it's quite painful, but it can be done. There is hope and there is a future for you. Even if you don't believe this now, we hope that by the time you've read and reread this book, you will.

This is your book (unless it's the library's, in which case you should run out and buy your own!). It's part of your personal grief pilgrimage. We want you to use it and make it yours. It's not bound in leather, and you're probably not going to keep it on your coffee table. So any book worth its salt is worth marking up. It's part of the way you digest what you read and make it yours. Underline the passages that are helpful to you. Star what you want to remember. Dog-ear sections that you want to come back to later.

You'll notice at the end of each chapter that there is a section called "Questions for Growth and Discussion." We encourage you to write your answers as you go along and to date them. Why date them? As you come back and read and reread this book, you'll be able to see how far you've come and how much you've grown! We encourage you to get together with a group of others who have lost loved ones. It doesn't have to be a big, formal group. One or two others will do. Go through the questions together and share and discuss them. You'll find this sharing to be immensely helpful as you go through this book and go through your grief.

This book cannot be digested in one gulp! It is intended to be read and reread. Not that it's long or profound or difficult. It's just that the first time through you might not be ready to grasp everything in this book. What you get will depend on where you are in your grief process. As you progress through your grief and come back and read and reread this book, you'll gain new insights and new help.

This book is written for all who have lost loved ones as well as for those who are trying to reach out and help friends who have lost loved ones. You will get different insights depending on where you're coming from. Much of our work has been with widowed persons, and as a result many of our illustrations will come from that perspective. Chapter 9 is the one chapter that's written primarily for those who have lost a spouse.

One word about words. We know many who aren't comfortable with the term "widowed," and sometimes we aren't either. We're not always comfortable with the word "bereaved" either. But we need to communicate, and they're the best words we could find. So we've used them.

We'd like to thank all of those who shared with us in our seminars, opening a part of their lives to us, sharing their joys and sorrows. They've given us a great deal and allowed us to pass it on to you. Thanks to William J. Downey of Wisconsin Memorial Park for encouraging us to minister in this area. Thanks to Dr. Basil Jackson, M.D., Ph.D., Th.D., for serving as Dick's doctoral adviser and for offering encouragement.

God loves you and we do too!

Richard Lewis Detrich
Nicola J. Steele

Littleton, Colorado

1

Take My Hand Through the Valley

E veryone at various times in life experiences loss. Loss is a part of life with which we must all painfully learn to cope. But not all losses are of equal magnitude. One of the most profound losses you can experience is the loss of one you love through death. The loss of a parent, a child, or a friend are all difficult; the more your identity was tied up in the life of the person whom you've lost, the greater your sense of loss will be. When we lose a parent, we are losing the one who gave us life, a name, and much of our self-concept. The loss of a spouse is particularly acute because your spouse is the person with whom you are most intimate and from whom you gain much of your identity. Even if a marriage survives all other pitfalls, it will eventually succumb to dissolution through death. To lose a child is most difficult because the child, regardless of age, is a part of the parent. This child is *my* child, *my* flesh, and it seems incredible that he or she is gone. We assume that parents are supposed to die first, and the loss of a child seems to violate the whole order of things.

The negative thinker looks at life and proclaims, "Living is dying," and in a sense he or she is right. Death is the end of life, and as such it is a part of life. Death is a universal human experience. Yet it is an experience of such finality that we can never be totally and absolutely emotionally prepared for its coming. Faith in the God of the Bible gives strength, comfort, hope, and the assurance of eternal life, but it doesn't prevent loneliness, fear, doubt, despair, and pain. Others want to help, and although they try, they cannot fully understand the confusing roller coaster of feelings the bereaved person feels. Emotions come like turbulent storms, frequently knocking you off balance. Frequently, you wonder if you are losing your sanity. When you are faced with the death of one you love, your world seems shattered. It is difficult to start picking up the pieces of a life which will never be the same. Familiar sights, sounds, and smells jar memories of the past. Feelings of guilt, anxiety, and anger erupt, leaving you bewildered.

Information helps to dispel fear. As you read this book, you will gain valuable information about what's happening to you. You need to know that grief is a time-consuming process. You don't recover overnight regardless of pressure from friends and relatives for you to do so. You need to know that your grief has certain recognizable stages: shock, suffering, acceptance, and growth. It's liberating to know that it's possible for you to grow, even through negative experiences, experiences which you wouldn't choose if you had the choice.

What Is This Pain Called Grief?

We asked that question of a group of bereaved persons at the beginning of a seminar. They used these words: "hurting," "sadness," "loneliness," "crying," "feeling inadequate," "bitterness," "anger." They were identifying feelings that are all a part of the process called grief.

"Grief is the feeling that you are dead inside. There's nothing there."

"Grief is being in limbo. If it wasn't for the kids and the dog, I probably wouldn't get up."

"Grief is not wanting to do anything. There's nobody to share it with."

"Grief is a time when your feelings are magnified all out of proportion. When a fuse blows, I'm ready to blow up the whole house."

Grief Work

Sigmund Freud first called this process "grief work." He wasn't kidding! This is the hardest work you'll ever be called on to do. Because grief is work, it requires a tremendous expenditure of emotional and physical energy. The work doesn't just happen. You can't stand idly by and expect your grief to work itself out. You have to be intimately involved in the process and work at it. Grief summons the whole range of your emotions, and that's exhausting!

How Long? How Long?

Grief isn't a single event in time but is a process. As such, it takes time, lots of time. We're all impatient with things that take time. We demand instant food, instant gratification, instant analysis, instant solutions to complex problems, and instant replays. We're impatient with a process that we can't speed up. It's the American way to find a faster way, but it doesn't work with grief! Grief, like growth, cannot be rushed.

Grief can last for years. We wish it didn't, but we feel it's better for you to know what you're facing from the start than to be misled or pushed to "hurry up" by others. The length of your grief depends on many things. Relationships are different, and so the length of grief is different. Each grief is unique and has special dimensions, but you should know that inside you is a timetable for your grief. It is uniquely yours. Your grief will take as much time as it will take, and nothing you can do will speed it up.

There is great pressure in our society for you to complete your grief and return to "normal" within a few months. Some succumb to this pressure, but don't you! One person said, "I've made up my mind in a few months that when people ask me how I'm doing, I'm going to say, 'Fine!' even if I don't feel that way." This is playing the game called "hide-and-seek"; you hide your true feelings to seek your friends' approval.

There used to be a time after the death of a loved one when people went into "mourning." At the time of the death a wreath was hung on the front door. This "mourning wreath" notified the community that things had irrevocably changed within the household. Women wore black clothing as an outward sign that they were in mourning. Because the family was in mourning, its members were exempt from certain social expectations. People generally remained in mourning until the first anniversary of the death. We think it's too bad we've dropped this custom, because it gave people time. People accepted without question that family members would be in mourning for at least a year, and the outward "mourning coat" reminded them of the fact.

Death usually happens in an instant. Even when there is a long, lingering illness or when death is slow and painful, at one moment the person is alive and at the next moment the person is dead (notable exceptions are when the brain dies before the body is allowed to die and when life-sustaining equipment is used to keep the person alive). Love does not die as quickly! A relationship which has taken years to build doesn't die in an instant. In a moment your loved one is gone, but your love is *not* gone.

Even after you've gone through the long, hard process of grieving, things don't return to "normal." Your loved one is gone and, at least from this side of heaven, is forever gone. Your life is fundamentally and radically changed. How can things ever be normal again? They can't! Life will never be the same again, but it can be good.

Don't Avoid the Pain

When anything is extremely painful, we try to avoid it. You may be tempted to avoid grief or attempt to shortcut it because it's so painful, but it is vital that you don't fight the process of grief. Participate in it fully. Don't avoid the painful feelings and emotions of bereavement. Unresolved grief is like a festering deep wound covered by a superficial scar. This kind of grief festers inside you and develops an infection which spreads and affects your entire emotional and physical self. There is a great mass of research that indicates that unresolved grief can produce a whole range of emotional and physical complications. So don't fight the process; go with it.

This Is a Time to Mourn

> There is a time for everything,
> and a season for every activity under heaven:
> a time to be born and a time to die,
> a time to plant and a time to uproot,
> a time to tear down and a time to build,
> a time to weep and a time to laugh,
> a time to mourn and a time to dance. . . .
> —Ecclesiastes 3:1-4, NIV

"Life belongs to the living" is a cliché of modern culture and indicates our aversion to death. The premise of our scientifically and technologically oriented society is that science and technology will ultimately conquer all, including death. The continuing intrusion of death into our lives is a nagging reminder of our failure. Death is an affront to our culture; so until very recently we have sought to deny the reality of death. People do not die; they "pass away." Friends try to hurry you through your grief and shield you from the reality of your loss. The day is long gone when family and friends constructed a pine coffin, prepared the body, carried it to the grave, lowered it into the ground, and shoveled the earth over their dead loved one.

Unable to handle the reality of death, we find it equally distasteful to deal with grief. We treat the wound of grief lightly, expecting that it should be healed within three to six months. When the grief persists, the bereaved person is challenged to "shape up" and "stop feeling sorry" for oneself, or perhaps it is politely suggested that the person has some psychological abnormality and he or she should seek professional help.

One widow observed, "Death has a way of showing us all how terribly vulnerable we are." But our modern society doesn't take to the concept of vulnerability. We like to think that we are invincible; yet death is a persistent, painful reminder of our vulnerability. When we're forced to confront the reality of death, we try to sidestep it by thinking, "Everybody dies sometime, but as for me ... not yet." Death is something off in the distant future, not something we contemplate as an always-present possibility. Yet death is a part of life. If we accept life we must also accept death. If you're not able to die, are you really able to live?

Getting Death out of the Closet

Every minute a death occurs in two American families. There are over six million widows in the United States alone. At any one time a million Americans are actively involved in the crisis of bereavement. Whereas death is final and certain and hence has a security of its own, bereavement is a continuing process. Since bereavement can be survived and is a repeatable experience, it is more common and perhaps more to be feared than death itself. You only die once, but you can suffer grief many times in a lifetime.

Largely through the pioneering work of Dr. Elizabeth Kübler-Ross, death has been brought out of the closet. In her work at Chicago's Billings Hospital with patients who were dying and in her subsequent work with health-care professionals, counselors, and clergy, Dr. Kübler-Ross has helped us confront the realities of death. While in the recent past children were routinely sheltered from death in our culture, death education is becoming an accepted inclusion in the curriculum of many schools. It is hoped that this increasing awareness of the reality of death will create a new attitude of understanding not only toward those who are dying but also toward those who are grieving.

Every human relationship is destined to end in a loss, at least this side of heaven. When speaking about loss, we always remember the comment of one woman who said emphatically, "I haven't lost my husband! I know where he is, and I'm going to see him again one day!" But loss this side of the grave is a price which must be paid for the joy of human relationships, a price brought about originally by humankind's sin and rebellion against God. *Loss* can be defined as being deprived of or without something or someone that you've valued and cherished. The sense of loss, or *separation,* is, of course, felt most keenly when you lose a person you have loved. At this time you suffer *bereavement,* which has been defined as the act of separation. This bereavement sets into motion a process called *grief.*

Well-Meaning Friends

Grief doesn't occur in a vacuum but in the midst of everyday life, and so it must involve friends, family, and neighbors. Grief cries out to be shared with another, but it is often hard to find the right person with whom to share. You need someone with whom you can be open, honest, and vulnerable. Someone who will take the time to listen, sometimes to the same things over and over. You need someone who's slow to give advice and easy answers. You need someone to encourage you gently but not prod or hamper you in the work of grief. It's hard for people looking on as bystanders to comprehend fully the depth of your grief. Family and friends may encourage you to become too dependent or, at the other extreme, not allow you any dependency.

Perhaps you've had complaints about well-meaning friends similar to these.

"People act as if my husband is no longer a part of my life just because he died. Even though my children are scattered around the country and I don't see them, they are part of my life. We shared a life together, and I need people to realize that experience is a part of my life."

"Some may say they know what you're going through, but they don't."

"Friends are going to listen once or twice on the phone, but that's it."

"Why do people I've known for years suddenly ignore me? I meet people in the grocery store, and they act like I have the measles."

"People will come at the time of the funeral and promise so much, but two or three weeks later, when you need them, they're nowhere to be found."

"The girls at work expect me to be the same as I was before. I may look the same, but I'm not. They don't realize that, or they don't want to."

We found this poem in *Woman's Day,* and although it refers to widows, we think that everyone in grief can identify with parts of it.

In the beginning
I would look at my watch and say,
"Yesterday he was here."

It has been a long time now since
I looked at my watch.
It has been so long
I do not even look at the calendar.

But in the beginning
People listened to each detail
As if listening confirmed their own mortality.
They were still here at the end of the story.
I guess fresh grief is like fresh milk:
We consume it quickly before it sours.

But grief cannot be worn
Season after season
Like a string of pearls.

Mourning becomes an embarrassment
To those who watch
The seasons of our sorrow.
A well-behaved widow
Does not cry.
(Me? Cry? Just because
I am lonesome for
The only man I ever loved?)

A good widow
Gets on with life.
(I brush my teeth and do not beat
My hands against the wall. I never look up
From my needlepoint and ask, "Why?")

A proper widow
Knows her place.
(Of course, I understand that
You will invite me to the *next* party—
The one with women only.)

A thoughtful widow
Makes no demands on children.
(I smile and tell them yes, go ahead,
I know you have your own life. I do not say,
"Once I had a life.")

I think now as I lie here in the dark
Of all the things we meant to do.
Alone they are nothing. But who wants
To listen to the solo song of widowhood?
No one but another widow, for she

Is the only one who knows the bitter truth.
It never gets better;
It only gets ordinary.[1]

Take My Hand Through the Valley

The psalmist wrote,

> The Lord is my shepherd, I shall
>   not want. . . .
> Even though I walk through the valley
>   of the shadow of death,
> I fear no evil;
> for thou art with me;
>   thy rod and thy staff,
>   they comfort me.
>   —Psalm 23:1-4

For years we've read this passage and thought that the psalmist was referring to the time when he would face death. We thought this passage was designed to assure us that God is with us even at the time of death. But now we look at it and realize that the psalmist was talking about grief, our grief. "Even though I walk *through* the valley of the *shadow* of death. . . ." The psalmist isn't dealing with facing the reality of his own death, but facing the death of another. He's walking *through* this time, and this time it's only a *shadow.* Even though he must walk through this difficult valley of grief, he fears no evil because he knows that God is with him. He's sure that even when all other comforts fail and helpers flee, God will be with him and sustain him and see him through the valley of his grief. And please note that you, like the psalmist, will get through.

You have a friend who will take you through the valley; his name is Jesus Christ. He says to you right now, "Take my hand through the valley. Walk with me, and we'll go through this grief thing together." He will see you through and bring you out on the other side!

It's comforting to know that Jesus knows the way through because he's been there before. He knows what grief is all about. Of all the accounts of grief in the Bible, one of the most poignant describes Jesus' visit to the home of his friend Lazarus just after Lazarus had died. The Bible tells us that Jesus sighed heavily and was deeply moved and wept. Not only has Jesus experienced grief, but he's also experienced death and come out on the other side of the grave alive! He knows the way through the valley, and he is going to guide you through. Reach out and grasp his hand!

[1] "The Widow," *Woman's Day,* February, 1978.

Questions for Growth and Discussion

1. In your own words how would you describe this experience of grief through which you are going?

2. How have you dealt with pressure from well-meaning friends for you to resolve your grief quickly?

Today's date: _____

Growth Challenge: Keeping a Journal

We've provided questions for growth and discussion at the end of each chapter. We encourage you to answer these questions and to write your answers down in this book and date them. After all, this is your book!

In addition, we'd like to ask you to keep a journal as you make your way through this book and as you work your way through your grief experience. Get a spiral notebook, a steno pad, or a "nothing book" (a bound book with blank pages sold in book or stationery stores). We want to encourage you to spend some time each day in silence and meditation. Maybe at the end of the day, perhaps at the beginning. We'd like you to jot down your real feelings in your journal; vent them; let them flow through your pen onto the pages of your journal. Keep your journal handy to grab at those times when you feel overwhelmed by feelings and emotions. You'll find this to be a helpful way of dealing with feelings. This writing isn't for publication. So don't worry about grammar and penmanship; just let it flow. A journal is a personal and private way of expressing your thoughts and feelings.

You'll find it helpful to be able to express yourself this way, and keeping a journal will play an important part in your grief recovery. Much later, when you look back and reread your journal, it will serve as a measure of how far you've come and how much you've grown. This will encourage you when you don't think you're making any progress.

2

Stages of Grief Work

The unknown is always more terrifying than the known. If you know what to expect in your grief process, the anxiety will be lessened. This chapter will help you understand some of the phases your grief will go through. But remember, since there is no one else on planet Earth quite like you, your grief experience is going to be uniquely yours. And yet there are some general stages that all grievers seem to go through in the process of their grief work.

Traditionally there have been three phases of grief, but we believe there is an additional stage of grief recovery; we call it growth. The growth stage of grief recovery is a lifelong process of personal stretching and development. It can be thought of as the reward at the end of the struggle. And it's so important that we've devoted an entire chapter to it (chapter 7).

As we see it, the four stages of grief recovery are

Phase One—Shock
Phase Two—Suffering
Phase Three—Recovery
Phase Four—Growth

So Many Loose Ends!

"It would be nice if the grief process were a little more predictable, without so many loose ends," said Fred after the death of his wife.

"I knew all about the stages of grief before Harold died," said Eleanor. "How come some of my reactions came as if I'd never heard of them before?"

In spite of the fact that we list four phases of grief, and they look nice and neat and orderly on the paper, don't expect them to be that way! They don't come in a nice, neat orderly progression. Each phase of grief has very ragged edges. At one moment you seem to be making some progress and moving from one phase into another, perhaps less painful phase. Then there is a flashback to the earlier, more painful stage. One woman compared her grief to a wild roller coaster ride. "I didn't want to get on, but I'm trapped, and it's running wildly out of control! Just when I think I'm getting better and coming up, the bottom drops out and I go plunging down to the depths again."

The pain always seems to be lurking around the fringes. Grief spirals down; it spirals up. Moods swing unpredictably. One day you're starting to feel like your old self again, and the next day you're in the pits of depression. Tears come without provocation. One widower expressed what's common to all grievers: "I'll be feeling fine, and then all of a sudden I'll be sitting at my desk crying. I don't know what triggers it; it just comes." This is the nature of grief.

"What's Happening to Me?"

You watch your moods swing. You feel as if you're losing or have lost control. You forget things. You have a hard time sleeping. You cook your husband's favorite meal and forget that he's not coming home to enjoy it. You wonder if you're losing your mind. We'll talk more about occurrences like these in chapter 6, "What's Normal and Abnormal in Grief." But you should know right now that reactions and sensations which otherwise might appear abnormal are perfectly normal in grief. The abnormal is normal when you're grieving. So concentrate on your grief work and try not to worry about the way you're feeling, acting, or thinking. It's all normal in this very abnormal process called grief.

How Long Is This Going to Take?

How long does it take? Just as long as it takes. A multitude of factors affect each individual's grief process; so there can be no set timetable for the process of grief. It takes as long as it takes. It can't be hurried. You can't hurry it along, nor can well-meaning friends who say, "Come on now! It's been long enough. It's time you started coming out of this!" Deep in your psyche is a timetable for your grief work, and nothing can speed it up. Take whatever time you need. Don't be hoodwinked into pretending it's OK when it isn't. This is going to be hard because most people who haven't experienced their own grief don't understand just how long it takes. But be assured that your healing will be most complete and your future will offer the most promise if you let your grief process consume all the time it needs. (There! We hope we just lifted *that* weight off your shoulders!)

Whenever we feel pain, we tend to want to resolve it as quickly as possible. We want to be done with it! Although the choice we make is not always a conscious one, we all make a choice as to how to resolve our grief. Some choose to get it over quickly and do anything that seems to make the grief go away—immediate re-marriage, moving, whatever. Others choose to allow themselves to work through their grief and go through the whole lengthy, painful process. At first, working through your grief seems the longer, more painful process. But you can't shortcut grief. Sooner or later unre-solved grief will return to haunt those who've tried to take a shortcut. Grief must be worked out, now or later, but *it must be worked out.* You can do it now, or you can do it later, but you will do it.

Jean's father lay dying in a hospital. He had been dying for a whole week. His condition seemed stable; so at dinnertime Jean left the hospital to prepare dinner for her children and put them to bed. Before she left, her father held her hand and begged her to stay. She said, "I'll be back just as soon as I fix dinner and get the kids to bed." While she was gone, her father died. Did he know he was going to die? Did he feel it? Is that why he begged her to stay?

Jean buried her grief, her should-haves, and her guilt, and didn't allow herself to go through much grief. Ten years later when her husband died, she was hit with a double dose of grief, and it was much harder to handle than it would have been had she worked through the grief from her father's death when it happened.

You see, it's best if you "allow" your grief. Don't fight it or push it, but allow your grief to work itself out according to its own timetable.

It is a mistake to think, as so many friends keep telling you, that "time heals all wounds." The loss of a spouse or any loved one is a permanent loss. Yes, the wound may heal in time, but the scar will always be there. In time you will learn to accept your loss, however reluctantly. You will grow through this experience, and someday you will once again feel like getting on with your life. But in the meantime, "It's as if my whole world has shattered," according to one woman. "And I don't think I'm ever going to get the pieces back together."

Or as Ella said, further along in her grief process, "Life will never be the same again, but . . . it can be good again."

Phase One—Shock

When death occurs suddenly, unexpectedly, accidentally, or violently, the impact of shock can be readily understood. But even when death is anticipated—long illness, hospital vigils, the opportunity to anticipate your loss—the actual death still produces shock. *Shock is defined as "a sudden or violent impact,"* and this provides an apt description of the initial phase of grief.

There isn't anything you can do to change the way in which you heard about the death of your loved one. But the way in which news of your loss is conveyed to you relates to how violently your body experiences shock. Particularly in the case of sudden, accidental, unexpected death, it is important that the news be conveyed with sensitivity and compassion.

Perhaps the person who told you about the death of your loved one tried to be sensitive and compassionate and did the best he or she could. Perhaps not. It's natural to be angry if someone told you about the death of your loved one without any sensitivity. But it might be helpful to you to understand that no one—police officer, foreman, doctor, or minister—likes to communicate news of a death. When we must tell another about the death of someone he or she loves, it hurts us, whether we try to cover up or not. We identify with the person's loss. We know it could have been our spouse, our child. We also know that we are mortal and vulnerable. We think, *It could have been me! It could have been my spouse standing there hearing that I am dead!* And that's very frightening to all of us. An academic degree, medical or police skill, theology, or whatever, doesn't take away that fear. For a doctor who's devoted his or her life to conquering death, the death of a patient is often seen as a personal defeat, as an assault on who he or she is as a person and as a professional.

Our purpose here is not to excuse but to help you understand. News of death should be communicated with understanding and compassion. People who are frequently called upon to communicate such news because of their professions should be trained in how to do it. We do this kind of training, and others do it too. If the person who told you about the death of your loved one didn't do it with sensitivity and compassion, you have every right to be angry, but it may help you if you seek to understand some of the inner confusion and anxiety that the person was feeling at the time.

Your reaction to the news of the loss of your loved one is shock. You can't believe it! This must be someone's idea of a sick joke. Why, you were just talking to your loved one, or only a few hours ago the two of you kissed good-bye. It can't be! This is a bad dream; you have to wake up.

Part of shock is an involuntary physical reaction. The impact of the news sends out immediate danger signals to your body, which reacts automatically in an effort to protect itself from further assault. Physiological reactions include rapid breathing, increased heartbeat, tensing of the muscles, sweating, dryness of the mouth, pain, nausea, involuntary bowel or bladder responses, and insomnia. All of these are normal responses over which you have no control. You may have experienced some or all of them.

There is a feeling of psychological and physiological numbness. You feel almost like a mechanical person going through the motions of making telephone calls, selecting clothes, and making funeral arrangements. You may have been up all night, maybe for weeks, and may be physically and emotionally exhausted. Sometimes you feel as if you're walking in a fog. When you look back on this time, you may not even remember what you did or how you got through those first agonizing days. Then, again, you may have recorded every detail as if it were part of a perverted, distorted Polaroid snapshot.

Many times people in shock react in ways that at other times would seem inappropriate or unacceptable. One teenager, whose brother had been stabbed, exploded in rage when told of the death, attacking the medical personnel in the emergency room and sending equipment and supplies flying. Some people become hysterical, sometimes crying, sometimes laughing. Any reaction, no matter how "abnormal," is normal in grief. Fortunately in this initial phase of grief, one is usually surrounded by understanding friends and relatives who do understand and readily forgive erratic behavior.

The loss of a spouse has been called a psychological amputation. Those who have had limbs amputated sometimes report a phenomenon called "phantom limb," in which they have sensations and still feel pain where their amputated limbs used to be. Widowed people frequently have a similar reaction to their psychological amputation, the loss of their spouse. Perhaps you've found yourself imagining that your spouse is still alive, expecting your spouse to return at any moment, and even setting the table for the one who is gone. All perfectly normal. Amputees also report vivid dreams in which they still have the lost limb. Some widows and widowers have vivid, intense, and sometimes sexual dreams in which the lost spouse is very much alive.

Your relationship didn't happen overnight but grew slowly through a period of dating and then through years of marriage. This relationship took years to develop, and the feelings don't just stop because your spouse is gone. It takes a long time to accept the reality of your loss.

We've said that you can't put a time frame on the phases of grief. The process takes as long as it takes. But just about the time your friends start to think that you're doing well and begin to expect you to start "coming out of it," that is about the time the bottom drops out. When everyone thinks you should be recovering nicely, the shock begins to wear off, and the enormity of your loss hits you full force. At this point you enter into the darkest and most painful phase of grief.

Phase Two—Suffering

You begin to move from the shock phase into the suffering phase when you realize that your loved one is not coming back, that life is never going to be the same again, and that this grief work is going to take a long, long time and be very painful. The shock wears off, and the full realization of your loss hits you like a sledgehammer. The painful second phase of grief is fittingly called *suffering.* It is suffering as you have never known before, unless you've gone through this grief work before. Even if you have grieved before, it won't be any easier this time. In fact, it may be worse. You will not only be suffering your present loss, but you will also be reliving, in a sense, the pain of your previous loss.

It is important during this phase of grief that you yield to the process of grieving and not fight it. Perhaps up to this time you haven't really let yourself go because you've been in shock. Your friends have said, "You're doing so well! You're holding up so well!" But sometimes you'd like to let it all hang out. And that's what you should do. Unresolved grief can have even more painful consequences than the pain of suffering and working through your grief. Feelings exist; they cannot be denied. The feelings of grief are real, and you must deal with them. It is important that you let those feelings flow and not suppress them. All of your feelings are important. They are normal, and they need to be expressed.

We've encouraged people to keep a journal during this period. You can use an old loose-leaf binder or a spiral notebook or steno pad. It doesn't have to be fancy; the important thing is that you use it. It's not for publication or sharing with others, but it's your own private journal, your record of your feelings and suffering. We've encouraged people to make a time each day when they record their thoughts and feelings in their journal. Imagine that your pen is the nozzle of a garden hose. When you sit down at your journal, you open the nozzle and allow the feelings to flow freely onto the paper. It will help you work through your grief if you can get all of these feelings out—the good, the bad, and the ugly feelings. Remember: feelings are! Don't think, "Oh, I shouldn't feel that way." You *do* feel that way! And expressing your feelings on the pages of your journal is a good way to deal with them.

You'll want to keep your journal handy for those times when the feelings—be they feelings of sadness, anger, guilt, whatever—build up within you and you need some release. Grab your journal and let it flow!

One of the helpful things about keeping your own personal journal is that it provides you with a record of your growth through your grief. There will be times when you'll be discouraged and think you're not getting anywhere. Times when your grief seems like a life sentence. Then it will be helpful for you to pick up your journal and read back through your entries. You'll be amazed at how far you've come, at how much you've grown, and it will give you encouragement to go on and work through your grief.

There is a period during this second phase of grief when you will feel a sense of utter despair and hopelessness. You will think that there is no future, at least not for you. A widow in our seminars challenged, "The future? What future?" A man said, "I never thought I'd have such a loss—that my life would have no meaning." But it is through the suffering that hope and life come. There will come a time when you start to come up out of the valley of your grief. A time when the ground under your feet starts to slant upward. There will come a time when you realize that however great your loss, you are alive, and you have a future. It is then that you begin to move into the next phase of grief.

Phase Three—Acceptance

Bob's wife was killed in a plane crash. He said, "I feel like I've lost two-thirds of myself, like there's only a third of me left." Most people who lose a spouse feel that a part of them has been torn away leaving a ragged, open, painful wound. The beauty of a healthy and growing marriage relationship is the unity and oneness that develop. The Bible speaks of this unity in terms of "one flesh." There is a unity, a "gluing" (the literal meaning of the Hebrew term for "one flesh"), a bonding that develops. This is what makes a good marriage relationship so great! But this is also what makes the loss of one's mate so devastating.

Once you have faced the enormity and reality of your loss and suffered through the impact of that reality, you can begin to move on into the third phase of grief recovery, that of gradual *acceptance* of your loss. Underline "gradual"! You don't wake up one morning and say, "OK, I accept it; now let's get on with life." Slowly you come to accept not only the fact of your loss but also the fact of your own continuing, albeit diminished, existence.

It is a *gradual* process. We like to use the illustration of a light bulb hooked up to a rheostat. At first there is only a tiny amount of current flowing, and the orange glow of the filament is barely perceptible. Gradually the current increases and the glow increases, and at some point you say, "The light is on." But *when* is it on? It's such a gradual process that it's hard to pinpoint when the light is on and when it's off. So it is with your grief. Your acceptance will be gradual; your belief in a future will be tentative. But if you go through the whole grief process and endure the pain, at some point the acceptance will come.

At this time Reinhold Niebuhr's familiar "Serenity Prayer" is very helpful. Stick it on your refrigerator and above your bathroom mirror. "God, grant me the serenity to accept the things I cannot change, the courage to change the things I can, and the wisdom to know the difference."

Part of the acceptance is not only to recognize the reality of your loss but also to be willing to *let go* of your lost loved one. This is the hardest part of grief. Many have said, "I can accept the reality of my loss, but I have such a hard time letting go." You are not alone in this struggle.

All of us think of our spouse as "my spouse," our children as "my children," our parents as "my parents." We think that somehow we can "own" another person. But that's really not possible. No matter how much we loved, no matter how deeply our lives intertwined, no matter what we shared, we cannot "own" another person. The person who is gone was never really yours but was always God's. The Bible says that that person was God's even before creation. God made that person, loved that person, and shared that person with you. (Thanks be to God! What a gift!) And the one whom you loved is God's now. God has promised to keep him or her until that day when we are resurrected to live together with God forever, reunited with those we love.

It is never easy to let go, and it is particularly hard to let go of a spouse. But in order to grow, we must let go. Letting go does not mean forgetting! Two lives touched! You and your spouse became one in the holy relationship of marriage. Your life is forever different, forever enriched, because of the relationship you shared with your spouse. Now your relationship has been broken, and you must let go of, but never forget, your loved one who has died.

Letting go is hard to do! It will take time, but it is a necessary part of your healing. As a Christian you are not letting your loved one go into oblivion, but into the arms of a God who loves you and loves the one whom you love.

Because of the ragged edges of the phases of grief, there will be times, even after you have come to accept the loss of your spouse and let go, that you will experience a flashback into the suffering phase.

Grief is not like this:

Rather, it is like this:

Anniversaries, birthdays, and holidays are particularly difficult. The anniversary times may be your wedding date, your loved one's birthday, the anniversary of the death, or even the time of year you met. It is helpful if you view these anniversary dates as times of thanksgiving for having been able to share the life of the person who has died. On holidays it is helpful to focus on the meaning of the holiday. You don't have to be ecstatically happy in order to appreciate the meaning and significance of holidays. It is sometimes helpful to plan ahead for holidays and think through your feelings in advance in order to devise a holiday observance that will be meaningful and helpful. Anticipate the holidays. Don't let them catch you by surprise!

Tom and Sharon never had any children; so it had been just the two of them on holidays. Christmas had been a special time for them, and they had shared their gifts in a way that was especially meaningful to them. On the first Christmas after Sharon's death, Tom was invited to spend Christmas day at his brother's. He carefully considered the invitation and pondered how he could best celebrate the holiday. The plan he decided on was to drop off his gifts for his brother's family the day before Christmas and pick up his gift. On Christmas morning Tom stayed home, thought about his wife, and let his feelings flow freely. He realized how much he missed her and how grateful he was for the time they had shared together. Christmas afternoon, after his brother's family had already opened their gifts, he went to his brother's house for dinner. It was a very meaningful day for Tom because he had planned ahead. Don't be afraid to be assertive! Celebrate the holidays in the way that is best for you, and don't let your friends push you into things you're not ready for or things you don't want to do. It's part of your healing; so be assertive and do what *you* want!

Christmas is always a difficult time. Over the years we've created a cultural myth, which we gorge commercially each year, that Christmas is a time of happiness, good cheer, family, and friends. We feel guilty, upset, and cheated if, because of our grief, we don't experience the orgasm of happiness that seems to be expected. But Christmas is, after all, a time of holy days and not a happy daze. The meaning of Christmas is in the event, in the coming of Christ into our world and into our lives. Focus on that event. Christ wasn't born at a party or even a family reunion, but in a stable, with few other people around. Planning ahead and focusing on the meaning of Christmas will help you through this difficult time.

In the acceptance phase of grief you begin to realize that life is going to go on. You do have a future. It will be different, but it can be good. You realize that there are many options open to you, many decisions that need to be made. This is the time to begin making decisions—sell the house? move?—but not before. You realize that whether you are thirty-six or seventy-six, you have a whole lifetime ahead in which to make these decisions and you needn't be rushed into any of them.

Phase Four—Growth

We believe that another stage of grief recovery needs to be added to the three traditional stages. As we talk with people who lost loved ones ten, twenty, thirty years ago, we're impressed that the process of grief continues. It changes; it becomes less painful, but it doesn't end. Sadie told us twenty years after her husband died, "They say that time heals, but that isn't entirely true. I mourn my husband's passing every day—to myself."

The *growth* stage of grief is a lifelong process of growth and development. Whether you realize it or not, you've been growing through your grief process all along. The fourth stage of grief is the light at the end of the tunnel. It's the reward for all the work you've done. When you look back, when you read through the entries in your journal, you'll realize not only how far you've come but also how far you can grow from here! We'll devote an entire chapter, chapter 7, "Growing Through Grief," to this fourth phase.

Questions for Growth and Discussion

1. How was the news of the death of your loved one communicated to you? How did this contribute to your grief work? How could it have been communicated more sensitively and compassionately?

2. Generally, in what phase of grief work are you now? How have you experienced the "ragged edges" of the phases of your grief?

3. What are some of the ways in which your spouse's life touched yours and in so doing made you forever a better person?

Today's date: _____

3

Anger and Grief

A nger. It comes in many ways, at many different times, and in many different intensities. Sometimes it is upsetting to be so angry and tiring to be angry for so long. It's easy to wonder, "What's the matter with me? I'm angry at everything and everyone. It just isn't natural and I'm tired of it!" Well, it is natural and it's very normal, particularly in grief. Not everyone feels angry, but many, many people do. It's OK to feel angry. Remember: *feelings are neither right nor wrong; they just are.*

It's OK to Feel Angry

JoAnne said she was always angry. She got up angry and went to bed angry. At times even her dreams were angry. JoAnne felt anger toward the doctor, the ambulance driver, even her neighbor's husband, who was still alive and who JoAnne thought was somewhat of a bum compared to her husband. She was angry at her niece who appeared to be wasting her life. She became livid when a dog dug in her flower bed and ruined some flowers. People who didn't do things right made her angry. She was even angry at God for taking away a very talented man with much to offer. JoAnne couldn't understand why God had given her husband such talent and then not allowed him to use it. Sometimes she got mad at her husband for leaving her with bills she couldn't pay and a car she knew nothing about and, most of all, for abandoning her with two little boys to raise. It all seemed too complicated and frustrating to bear. JoAnne was very tired of being angry all the time. Even when things seemed to be going smoothly, something minor would set her off again. One time the kitchen sink clogged up. Ordinarily she would have poured something down the drain or plunged it out. For some reason she couldn't figure out what to do, and that made her angry at herself. She felt she wasn't holding things together the way she should.

A friend commented at one point that JoAnne had changed into such an angry person that it was uncomfortable to be around her. "Isn't it time you got ahold of yourself?" the friend asked. The comment was upsetting. JoAnne thought, "She's right! I'm angry so often that maybe I should stop being angry. It can't be normal to be this angry. I need all the friends I've got, and I don't want to risk losing them." So JoAnne worried about her anger and tried to control it, but it wouldn't go away. She felt angry. Period.

You may or may not feel as angry as JoAnne. However you feel, understand that anger is a very real part of grief. It's strange that although we talk about anger a lot in our society, we're uncomfortable being around people who are angry; we ourselves don't like to be angry. "Proper" people don't express their anger. We're afraid that if we let people see how angry we are, they, too, might leave us. Also, we're afraid of what we might do if we should get really angry.

Almost Everyone Gets Angry

Closely related to the word "grieve" is the word "grievance," which the dictionary defines as "being in a state of anger." Corporations realize that if they want their organizations to run smoothly, angry employees must have somewhere to take their anger. So they have grievance boards, or what you might think of as "anger boards," so that the anger can be *expressed, dealt with,* and *resolved.* Only then can their employees return to work *effectively.* If the anger is ignored and nothing is settled, the feelings continue to rumble around, grow, pop out at inappropriate places, and negatively affect the employee's work. Anger needs to be recognized. If it is important enough for *companies* to recognize the fact that anger "is" and needs to be dealt with, it is equally important for *us* to recognize the fact that anger "is." It won't go away just because we wish it would. Anger is a part of grieving.

Almost everyone gets angry at some point after the loss of a loved one. The person who died was a very important part of your life. You've changed because of that person. You're different because that individual came into your life. In many respects you truly became "one." So when that person is ripped from your life, there is a large, gaping hole. You feel invaded, and the invasion leaves you vulnerable. It's normal to be angry when something or someone important to you is taken away.

When our daughter Noelle was about a year old, the grocery store clerks and bank tellers began giving her suckers as a treat. We didn't want her having unnecessary candy; so our war with the system began. At one point Nikki had had enough. When a clerk gave Noelle a sucker without bothering to ask, Nikki quickly grabbed it away. Noelle put up such a fuss, screaming and crying, that everyone in the store came to see what was the problem. Noelle was furious that the sucker she had had for about three seconds had been taken away from her. All that commotion for a sucker! Children have pure, raw emotions. They haven't learned all the social amenities for dealing with anger. They haven't learned the controls. What they feel automatically comes out.

When someone you love is torn away, the experience leaves an open, gaping hole. All the controls and the veneer of "proper social behavior" don't work anymore. The raw emotions come through, often with very little censoring. If there is anger, it will come out—and it needs to come out. You can't hold it in. If you do, it will come out in other, destructive ways, including physical illnesses.

When emotions are raw and right out front, it's best to acknowledge them. We know we're angry and so does everyone else. The question is "What do we do about it?" The easiest, and also the hardest, thing is to accept that the feelings are there and to go ahead and express them. Don't let anyone take the feelings away or make you feel guilty about having your feelings. If you're angry, be angry. That's OK! Expressing your anger is the quickest way to be rid of it. The idea is to get rid of it by releasing it and not to swallow your anger and let it fester. Don't let anger build up inside you. You just don't have enough physical and emotional energy to deal with pent-up anger in addition to everything else.

"Why Do Things That Ordinarily Wouldn't Be Overwhelming Seem to Be Such a Big Deal?"

There seems to be much that produces anger in grief, and like other emotions of grief, the anger seems bigger than life. You wonder why things that ordinarily would not be any big deal suddenly seem overwhelming. Any other time you might have been glad to bake a cake for charity. Now it seems like an intrusion and too much to ask. A bill comes in the mail that you normally would have paid immediately. Now, with your concern about finances, that bill becomes a mountainous hurdle. Stubbing a toe can cause buckets of tears. At another time these things wouldn't be so upsetting, but remember, in grief work the abnormal frequently becomes normal. What's wrong with you? Nothing. Right now emotions just seem larger than life.

Because our emotions are raw, things will seem larger than life for a while. It is easy to feel hurt and angry. It seems that relatives and friends who've always cared for us can hurt us more readily than before. Words meant to console can make us angry. "Be glad it happened quickly; he didn't suffer." Certainly such words are logical, but the anger asks, "Why now, when we had so many plans?" "Why me? I needed her so badly, and she hadn't begun to live yet." "Why him? He was such a good man, such a loving husband and father." Or someone will say, "At last he has peace after a long suffering." Yes, logically that may be true. But our anger asks, "Why did he have to endure suffering in the first place?" A friend says, "Knowing that he was going to die must have made it easier for you to be prepared." The anger says, "How can you say that when I hurt so much? It isn't easier! Don't you know how much grief there is in knowing?"

Our society doesn't know how to deal with anger, and it certainly hasn't trained us to do so. Anger can be frightening because we don't know where it will take us, what will happen, or if it will ever end. We don't feel as if we can control it. But that's OK because control isn't always the answer. We need to learn ways to release anger effectively. Some are included at the end of this chapter. Experiencing your anger and understanding it as part of your healing are the keys. If your anger becomes destructive, then by all means seek some outside counsel. But otherwise understand that it is part of your healing.

Free-Floating Anger

Has anyone ever asked you what or whom you were angry at? Your reply might be, "No one in particular. Everyone! I don't know." This is called "free-floating anger." Anything can set you off. Such feelings can seem irrational to others and sometimes even to ourselves.

Marilyn went to the bank one afternoon to cash a check. The day was beautiful. She was the only customer in the bank, and the teller was pleasant and unhurried. As the teller was counting Marilyn's money, she answered the telephone, counting and talking on the phone at the same time. It didn't work. She counted incorrectly and had to begin again. Marilyn became furious. She lashed out at the teller for trying to do two things at once and being inept at both. Through gritted teeth she pointed out that there were five other people who could have taken the call. Marilyn knew her response was irrational, and she felt as though she'd made a fool of herself; so she fled in tears with her money. She was very upset with herself and kept berating herself for getting angry over nothing. She told a friend, and the friend agreed that Marilyn's reaction had been pretty extreme. That made Marilyn feel even worse.

It's common not to have any real focus for your anger. It blurts out quickly at whoever happens to be there. So you get angry at the grocer, a friend, the bank teller, your insurance agent, the paper boy who throws the paper in the flowers—the list is endless. The feeling of anger is there, and when we find a target, any target, it just pops out. It's frustrating, annoying, embarrassing, and at times frightening. You don't like being this way or having others see you this way. You've lost your loved one, and you don't want to lose your friends as well.

If you can understand that these feelings of free-floating anger are part of your grief work, you won't be as frustrated by them or feel as powerless. It will be easier to say, "I'm not sick or acting strange," and then apologize to friends and explain to them that these feelings exist and need to be expressed. It is far better to get the feelings out, even if you don't do it in the best way, than to swallow them. This is not the time to worry about what Emily Post or anyone else might think. As time passes, you'll be better able to deal with your anger. Right now those emotions are too raw and too difficult to control. You just don't have the energy to deal with all the I-should-haves and I-shouldn't-haves. You need to understand this fact, and your friends need to understand it, too.

Direct Anger

In addition to free-floating anger, there is also direct anger. Direct anger might be toward the doctor, nurse, minister, funeral director, your children, or relatives. Sometimes you feel that they have been negligent in their responsibilities. They could have done more or been more aware. The pastor should have come when you called and stayed with you during those diffficult hours. Or he or she should have left you alone. The nurse should have called sooner and told you to come to the hospital before your husband died. The cleaning person should have stayed out of the hospital room and not made so much noise.

According to LaVerne, the doctor didn't seem concerned about the contraindications of drugs being given to her husband. When he finally died, she was certain it was because of improper medication. She was angry at the doctor because she felt he should have checked on this. Even the nurses should have said something. LaVerne was also angry at herself for not getting another opinion or demanding that the medication be stopped.

Karen was extremely angry at the police for coming to her door and blurting out that her husband had been killed. She said they didn't give her any sort of warning. They didn't give her any time to prepare. "It was like a concrete wall smashing into me at one hundred miles an hour."

Because this type of anger has a direct target, you can deal with it if you decide to. After almost eight months Karen went to the police department and talked to the police chief about her feelings. LaVerne hired an attorney to investigate the specifics of her husband's case. Sometimes it helps to take a friend with you who understands the situation and knows exactly what you want to say. The friend can back you up, rephrase, and sometimes help you not to be railroaded into accepting an explanation you don't want to accept. Do whatever *you* need to do to resolve these feelings constructively. It might not be right away, but plan whatever action you need to take so that you don't swallow your anger but deal with it instead. Remember the illustration of the grievance board. When you find a way to express your anger and make an opportunity to deal with it, you can resolve the situation, put it away, and continue with your life.

Early in our grief we tend to become angry at the people who have the most contact with us or affect our lives the most. These are usually the ones closest to us. They may be our children. If they're small, sometimes they're an open irritation for our wound. We love them, but it's quite difficult to put up with their noise and their constant need for attention. It is very hard to recognize and deal with the problems *they* have in dealing with *their* feelings of loss. If they're older, they may resent *us*. We may be the focus of their free-floating anger. Or they may be overprotective and controlling of us. We may not feel that they are giving us the right amount or type of support.

Frequently in-laws are the target of anger. You may feel they wanted too much say about the funeral details or disposition of your loved one's things. All of a sudden they may seem to be everywhere and demanding, or they may seem to be nowhere when they should be helping and giving support.

During the first year of grief the resentment can seem to build while at the same time you struggle with feelings that "it shouldn't be like this." You want to find some normalcy and peace. You want things to settle down so you can have more consistent feelings. Often the people who should be helping you aren't. You have every right to feel angry; so go ahead and feel angry. Later on, when you want to, and when you have the energy to, you can always talk to the people with whom you're angry or confide in a close friend about the situation. But do get the anger out and deal with it so that it isn't eating at you for the rest of your life. You may not feel like dealing with the situation now, or next month, but at some point when you feel like taking action, deal with the situation. If it can be helped, don't leave this business unfinished.

"Would God Fall Apart If I Got Angry with Him?"

God is an ominous target for our anger. It's easy to think that if we dare get angry with God, there is the possibility of receiving divine anger in return, and what would that lead to? Many times we're angry at God but afraid to admit our anger or verbalize it.

Scientists tell us that the universe is eight billion light years across and that the heavens are alive with motion and change. The idea that the God who made all this, and is even now guiding and directing the universe and galaxies of space, could fall apart if we got angry is ridiculous. Yet a lot of us act as if anger directed at God would somehow make him fall apart or zap us with lightning. We're afraid to get angry at God; yet deep inside we do feel angry at God because of our loss.

God is big enough to take our anger and not fall apart! Sometimes in order to realize how big and great and good and loving God is, we need to get angry with him and confess that anger to him. Jesus cried out on the cross, "My God, why have you forsaken me?" Certainly that's the same cry of anguish and anger we sometimes feel. The psalmist cried out and wrestled with God, letting go of his feelings of hurt and anger. When we go to God and explain how angry we are with him, he listens, understands, accepts, loves, and wraps comforting arms around us. And when we've finished flailing our arms and our anger is spent, God wipes away our tears—and is still there. Listening to our anger is one of God's ways of helping our healing.

Becky, our two-year-old, is at times a very stubborn, headstrong, determined, and impatient little girl. Dick doesn't know where she gets those traits, but Nikki claims she knows. Sometimes when Dick tells Becky to do something and she doesn't want to do it, an irresistible force meets an immovable object—and the result is friction! Even though Becky throws a tantrum and screams and kicks, Dick doesn't stop loving her for a moment! He doesn't fall apart or overreact! And when she's exhausted and her anger is spent, Dick is still there to hold and comfort her.

God, our heavenly Father, has a wonderful plan for each of our lives. It's a plan for good and for fullness of life. But sometimes it's hard to see that plan. People tell us, "All things work together for good to them that love God" (Romans 8:28, KJV). We try to believe that, but often we feel like shouting, "What do you mean? It certainly isn't good for me." But sometimes in order to see that plan, in order to realize that God is in control and working out that plan, we need to let go and express our anger.

We can't fathom what God can fathom. We don't know what God knows. But nevertheless we can believe that God knows what is best for us and accept that. But sometimes along the way we're going to get angry at God. That's OK—God can take it! God is not going to fall apart! Sometimes we may even get angry and sin, but that doesn't make us any less loved, any less forgiven, or any less valuable in the hollow of God's hand. God in his own time and way is working out all things for our good. And through the anger and the tears, he's going to show us the plan.

When it doesn't seem that things are working out for your good, you need to understand where you are. Right now you're concentrating on the idea that things *aren't* working out for your good. That's part of the process. Right now you're a very egocentric person—and you *need* to be. Not that you purposely want to ignore or exclude others, but right now is the time when you really need to think, "I'm Number One and I'm looking out for Number One." It won't always be that way! But now you have an emotional wound that you must take care of if you want it to heal properly. It may look and feel as though you have blinders on and aren't concerned with anyone or anything else. It won't always be that way, but it must be that way now. God understands this. He's the one who gave our bodies and our emotions the ability to heal if we follow the process. And when our prayers don't seem to reach even the ceiling and we don't get anything out of church, God understands. These feelings are part of being totally absorbed in ourselves for the moment. It won't always be this way! Our energies automatically go inward; so it's hard to propel a complicated prayer very far. Sometimes "Help!" is the only prayer we can utter. But God hears, understands, and answers nevertheless. Rarely does a typical church service meet us exactly at the point in our grief where we are at the moment. But eventually, in time and without pushing, we'll be able to pray the way we used to and find meaning in worship.

"Could I Be Angry At . . . ?"

"Could I be angry at the loved one who has died?" Yes, it's OK to be angry at the person who has died. No relationship is perfect. You were sometimes angry at that person when he or she was alive; so why should you no longer be angry just because he or she has died?

Nikki worked with a program for drug addicts in a psychiatric hospital. One day the staff members were discussing the feelings they had about a young drug addict who had committed suicide. Many emotions were being shared, which gradually led to a discussion of death in general. One of the psychiatric nurses began to talk about her husband, who had died almost twenty years earlier, and how difficult it had been for her to raise her two daughters without his presence and support. She had talked freely of him but always with the phrase "He left me." With a little prodding she began to talk of her anger at his leaving. She began to unearth feelings that had been buried for years. It became so real to her that his death seemed like yesterday; for the first time in almost twenty years, she was able to verbalize her anger at her husband for dying and leaving her. For twenty years she'd swallowed her anger, feeling that it wasn't right to be angry. Her husband was dead and couldn't defend himself. Plus the fact that her anger wasn't logical. Her logic told her that he couldn't help dying. But, as we've said before, grieving isn't a time to be logical. It's a time when emotions and feelings take over and demand to be expressed. Deal with them now, or deal with them later, but you must deal with them. It's easier, and it speeds your healing if you deal with them now.

In the past if you had found out that your finances were a mess or your children were misbehaving and having problems, and your mate wasn't around, you would have been angry. So now that your spouse is gone if you find out that the finances are a mess or the children are missing his guidance, why not be angry now? It doesn't have to be logical. *Feelings are!* Express the feelings. Your memory of your loved one will be clearer because you've washed away the feelings and the emotions that are blurring the memory. After you deal with the feelings of anger, you can better focus on the feelings of love, which are better than anger.

Believe That You Can Get Through

A pilot took off in a single-engine plane from an airport on a beautiful day. All of a sudden the clouds covered him. The way was obscured by lightning and thunder and dense clouds. It was terribly frightening. The pilot knew he couldn't turn back. All he could do was to keep flying through the storm, trusting and believing that he would come out on the other side of the storm to greet the sunshine. The storm beat on the small plane and threatened to tear it apart, but the pilot kept his course. He didn't give up; he believed he would get through. And he did!

Grief is like that. The ominous feelings of anger are like that. You can't deny them; they're there. You can't turn back or run from them, or you'll crash. You just have to go on through the storm, keeping on course and trusting that you will get through and find sunshine and hope after the storm.

"How Do I Cope?"

The emotions of grief are a little like the game of racquet ball. The emotions are flying in all directions, going so fast and ricocheting here and there that at times you just want to yell, "Stop!" You want desperately to find calm and peace at a time when your feelings are terribly confusing.

One moment we feel like shutting down in order to find some calm. The next moment we're striking out and thrashing about. Or we're hanging on tight hoping that we'll get some control and be able to deal with the roller coaster of feelings. It's confusing and hard to know how to cope.

The most productive way of dealing with feelings is always to think "outward." Emotions have to go somewhere, and it's better to direct them outward than inward. If you keep thinking *outward,* you'll be better able to direct feelings into some satisfying forms of expression. When you play cards, if you keep your cards within an inch of your chest so that no one else can see them, you have a difficult time seeing them also. You won't know which card to play because you won't know what you have. If you hold them out, you can see them more clearly and understand how to utilize them. If your emotions are out where you can see them, you can cope with them more easily and can gain a greater sense of control.

So think *outward.* Relax. Let what emotions come, come. They may not all come this week or even this month, but when you feel them, let them out.

How to Deal with Anger

"How do I deal with my anger?" Since you've been taught for much of your life not to express anger, you may find it hard to get it out even when you know you must. You're probably not used to dealing with so many emotions at once and find it all tiring and confusing.

Here are some suggestions in dealing with your anger constructively.

1. *Repeat in your mind that feelings are.* Feelings are neither right nor wrong; they just are. That includes anger. So it's OK to feel angry.

2. *Direct your emotions outward rather than inward.* Talk, talk, talk. If you're afraid of losing friends (and many friends don't want to listen all the time), sit down with those you feel you can depend on and explain to them how important it is for you to talk and get your emotions out. Tell them what responses you'd like from them. Some friends turn you off simply because they don't know how to respond. Talk to them in a quiet, unpressured moment when you won't be interrupted so that you can find out how they feel about this. Do this with several friends—the more the better.

Find a support group within your community. Participating in such a group is one of the best ways to be able to talk and feel that someone else in a similar situation knows exactly what you mean. Whether the time lapse for you has been two weeks or two years, a support group will be helpful. It's part of your healing. If you broke your leg, you might very well get some of the most helpful, practical information from someone else who had done the same thing. A bond of similar experience can be very helpful.

If friends are few and/or you don't want to talk to them, talk to a tape recorder, write in your journal, talk to your cat or dog. Talk to anything or anyone you feel comfortable talking to, but talk!

3. *Repeat to yourself that it's OK to be angry.* You can be angry at whomever you want—the doctor, the minister, the one who has died, or God.

4. *Find several things that help you feel release in directing your anger (or other emotions) outward.* Always have a plan in mind and a backup plan. If Plan A doesn't work this time, you have plans B and C ready to roll. When you plan ahead for safe ways to let out your anger, you don't have to try to think of them when the need arises. You can feel more in control because *you* have chosen the direction for your own feelings.

Some ideas:

- Jog.
- Hit a pillow.
- Get a plastic baseball bat and hit the bed.
- Buy some old, rummage-sale dishes to smash. (Can't you just see yourself? It may sound weird, and you may end up laughing after the release, but it's a lot better than keeping the anger bottled up inside, isn't it?)
- Clean or paint something, or mow the lawn. (One woman volunteered to lay sod for a landscaper!)
- Pound on a piano.
- Find a good place to scream. (A car in a deserted place with the windows rolled up works well. The basement is good if you warn the neighbors beforehand so that they won't be alarmed.)
- Play tennis, soccer, racquet ball, or any game in which you hit or kick a ball.
- Listen to the 1812 Overture turned to as high volume as possible.
- Listen to the 1812 Overture turned to as high volume as possible—while throwing dishes.
- Don't be afraid of seeing a counselor for suggestions.

5. *Understand that intense feelings like anger can be handled in these ways: expressed, suppressed, repressed, and confessed.*

Express: to get your feelings out in the open and rid yourself of them; to help others understand how you feel.

Suppress: to consciously and deliberately push down the feelings so as not to let them get out. This process is similar to packing a suitcase. You keep putting things in and then try to close it by sitting on it. But give that suitcase a little outside pressure, perhaps a bump in the wrong place, and it will explode. Everything will come flying out. A suitcase is meant to handle only a certain amount and can't be expected to handle twice as much without something drastic happening. The same is true of you and your emotions.

Repress: to unconsciously push your too-painful feelings deep into your subconscious because you can't deal with them. Eventually they will push their way out of hiding, perhaps errupting in unhealthful ways.

Confess: to admit to God the way you feel, even if you think you shouldn't feel the way you do. Some feelings cannot be expressed. Repressing or suppressing these feelings is like having a wound that has been improperly cleansed. On the outside the wound looks as though it is healing, but inside it is infected. In order to promote healing, you must cleanse the wound. That's what confession can be. Confessing to God helps you to cleanse the wound and enables you to be forgiven and to forgive yourself.

The two most important people in your confession are you and God. God in divine power will forgive, and it's in the depth of this forgiveness that you can find the power to forgive yourself, cleansing and starting the healing of your wound. If others won't forgive, that's their problem, not yours. If they are unable to forgive you, they must work that through as a part of *their* healing. But at least you've done your part for *your* healing.

6. *Anticipate a positive outcome.* Expect it, plan for it, and it will happen.

Questions for Growth and Discussion

1. What have been sources of anger for you throughout your grief?

2. Do you feel changes in your anger?

3. Do you feel you are dealing with your anger productively or are you still overcome by it?

Today's date:_____

4

Guilt and Grief

Have you ever taken a coat off the hanger and turned it inside out before putting it on? (Not a reversible coat.) Of course not! That's not how the coat is meant to be worn. Turned inside out it is uncomfortable, doesn't button properly, looks bad, and generally doesn't function as intended.

Guilt is the coat of anger turned inside out. Anger directed outward can be released and gotten rid of. Anger turned inward upon ourselves can become guilt. It hampers us, bogs us down, and can be very uncomfortable. Like the coat, anger is not meant to be turned around. That's why the previous chapter on dealing with anger is so important.

Often we feel angry at ourselves for something we did or did not do. Instead of getting that anger out and dealing with it, we turn it inward, try to ignore it, and hope it will go away. But it doesn't. It becomes guilt. Like anger, guilt will not disappear just because we wish it away. It must be acknowledged and dealt with. Sometimes we can deal with it as we work our way through grief and sort through our feelings, but sometimes it takes the help of a trained counselor to pry out the feelings and be done with them. Guilt can cripple and prevent healing from taking place. It can be one of the biggest hurdles in getting through grief.

Although some guilt is normal, it is still one of the most painful aspects of our grief. We feel that we were somehow responsible, that we could somehow have prevented the death of the one we love. While guilt is a normal part of grief, it can also be abnormal. The difference between normal and abnormal is how we handle our feelings of guilt.

There are primarily two kinds of guilt associated with grief. One is guilt over aspects of the relationship which were not what they might have been: deeds done, words spoken, arguments and disagreements left unresolved by death. The other kind of guilt has to do with circumstances surrounding the death of the loved one.

Guilt over Less-than-Perfect Relationships

"If Only. . . ."

It is important to understand that no relationship is perfect. In every relationship there are aspects that are not what we want them to be. Even in good relationships there are disagreements and arguments. We fight, argue, disagree. Part of our development as individuals and part of the building of a relationship requires that we have and express a full range of emotions. These emotions help us grow, expand, and develop. We use them to test limits and set boundaries for ourselves and others. That's what makes relationships alive. If we didn't use all these emotions, a relationship would be dull and one-dimensional. We may not always like how we handle the feelings or what we do to one another, but the whole range of feelings is part of our learning and struggling to develop our relationship and love. It's part of being "we."

Sometimes we say things that slip out in the heat of the moment, and at other times we want to hurt. Usually we think, "At some point we'll resolve this, but right now I'm just angry." And ordinarily we do settle it in some way. Maybe not always the way we'd like, but at least there is some resolution.

This time the disagreement was not settled. Our loved one died before we could resolve the issue. Thoughts cross our minds like, *If Harry hadn't stormed out of here so mad at me, would he still have had the accident?* We wish, *If only I could have told him one more time that I loved him. It was such a stupid, silly, little thing.* And that stupid, silly, little thing stands unresolved and becomes a big mountain of guilt.

If only we knew when life would end, there would be many things we would do differently. But we can't always tie things up in nice, neat little packages in life. Many times there are loose ends. This time there was no resolution, no being "together."

You have already set a pattern for taking care of disagreements in your relationship. If your loved one had not died, you would have taken care of this someday, just as you'd always done before. The feelings you built in your relationship haven't ended at death. In your own mind you can resolve the disagreement and in time find some peace about it. We suggest that you write a letter to the one who has died. Sit down, and write just what you would say to him or her if he or she were here. Explain what happened. Ask for the person's forgiveness. You can keep the letter or destroy it, but you'll find that it helps you to verbalize what you would say and imagine what the one who has gone would say. It helps you feel his or her forgiveness and makes it easier for you to forgive yourself.

"I Should Have. . . ."

After his heart attack, Mary was always telling her husband not to mow the lawn and weed the garden. And he was always telling her it was good therapy, he enjoyed it, and he found it relaxing. One morning after the one hundreth conversation like this, Mary found her husband in the garden. He had suffered another heart attack and died. Rather than focusing on the fact that he had made the choice and that he had died doing something he enjoyed, Mary berated herself for not forcing him to hire someone to do the gardening, for not checking him often enough, for not making him take a break. "I wasn't adamant enough. I knew this could happen!"

Jean's father was in the hospital for a long time. She faithfully went to see him every day. One evening he asked her to stay longer than usual. He said he was afraid to die and didn't want to be alone. Jean said, "You're not going to die! I'll be back as soon as I fix dinner." As Jean walked into her home, the phone began ringing. The nurse on the other end told her that her father had just died. She felt guilty. "If I only had listened to what he said and stayed another fifteen minutes, I could have been with him. I could have been there and helped him with his fear. I should have asked the family to go to McDonald's."

We all have our should-haves. You have yours. We'd all like to think that we have more power than we do. We like to think that we could have run our loved one's life better. But in Mary's case, her husband had made the choice to work in the garden. Responsibility doesn't mean making choices for another person. Loving is a give-and-take relationship. If you love someone, you don't try to run that person's life or take away his or her choices.

Jean had been seeing her father every day. She loved him and had tried to make his hospital stay as pleasant as possible. She could not have known that he was going to die when he did.

Esther, too, felt terribly guilty because she hadn't listened to her mother-in-law's advice to change doctors. If she had, maybe her husband would still have been alive. She carried this guilt for quite some time until a friend supported her in bringing her husband's case history to another doctor for review. He told her that it wouldn't have helped. There was nothing she could have done.

Snagged by a Moment

Many times guilt comes when we are "snagged by a moment." Rather than looking at the whole picture, rather than looking at all the facts, we become snagged by a single moment in time, a single action in which we feel we've failed. We focus and refocus on that single moment. We relive it and analyze it; we become snagged by it.

There is so much that we would change if "we had known," so many things that we would have tried differently. But the truth is that the outcome would probably have been very much the same. We are not God, able to foresee the future or control it. Life has risks. There are no guarantees. We try to do the best we can for the moment, based on the knowledge we have.

This is all realistic. It's logical. "Then why is it that I feel the way I do?" Because grief is not logical. It is emotional. That's why all the rational, logical answers of "You did all you could do" don't make you feel better. Particularly in the suffering stage, grief isn't conducive to logic. But it is possible—given time, given the insight that comes through time or research, given the ability to express guilt and anger—it is possible to understand. It is possible, eventually if not now, to understand and to work through guilt until you come to the conclusion, "I did everything that I could do. It was something over which I had no control." And so you are able to let go of your guilt.

"How Could You ... ?"

Sometimes friends and relatives can say something that makes you feel guilty. You snag onto something they say. A thought planted in your mind takes root and grows until you convince yourself it's true—even if it's not. Be careful to whom you listen. Don't let others judge you; during this period of your grief you're a hard enough judge on yourself. Remember that at this phase your grief work is consuming all of your energy and you don't have energy to defend yourself. If you don't like what you're hearing, don't listen. This is a time when you have to look out for you! Don't be afraid to be assertive in looking out for Number One, at least right now.

Janet's mother came to visit a few months after Janet's teenage son had been killed in a car accident. Janet was in grief, and her mother, who'd lost her favorite grandson, was also in grief. Part of grief is anger. In a misdirection of her anger, Janet's mother lashed out. "What kind of mother are you to let David go out at night when he had just learned how to drive? I raised seven and nothing happened to them!"

Janet's mother had set herself up as the perfect mother. Realistically Janet knew that wasn't so. But the idea began to work on Janet because grief is not a rational, logical time. Certainly, Janet knew that no parent is perfect. But when her own parent came along and planted that seed of doubt, guilt began to creep up on Janet. She began to think, "She was the perfect parent. She raised seven children. I couldn't even raise one. What a failure I am! How ashamed I am!"

When grief collides with grief, guilt can increase geometrically. Her mother made an accusation which touched a vulnerable place in Janet, a place of doubt, and Janet multiplied the accusation until it was out of control.

Many women have been schooled to feel guilty by articles and advertisements in women's magazines which say, "If you cook right and use the proper ingredients, you'll lengthen your husband's life." Because it was thought that cholesterol was the number one contributor to heart disease, the woman, who usually planned the menu and did the cooking, bore the burden for her husband's life or death—at least that's what the magazines led you to believe. Many women got snagged on this. "If I had loved him more, I would have been more careful. I would have watched his diet and learned more." Ironically, cholesterol, while still a contributing factor, is no longer looked on as a major cause of heart disease. It's sad to see people go on a guilt trip and then have the researchers turn around and say, "Sorry, we were wrong."

When you're able, and when you can think more logically and rationally, obtain whatever factual information you can get. Then don't let others lay a guilt trip on you.

How to Sort Out Guilt

Feelings of guilt are usually most intense during the suffering phase of grief, and the guilty feelings contribute to the suffering. As you move along in your grief work toward the acceptance phase, you'll be better able to sort through your guilt feelings and put things into a clearer perspective. The questions you're asking—"Should I?" "Could I?"—and the guilt you sometimes feel are, for the most part, normal expressions of grief. Don't squash your feelings. It's when you keep them pushed down that they can hurt you. Guilt feelings become an obstacle in grief recovery because people are hesitant to share them. Sharing feelings, getting them out, expressing them, writing them down in your journal—these are all helpful ways of sorting through your guilt. Don't be fooled into thinking, *In time this will go away.* You must work to be sure your guilt feelings are dealt with and resolved so that you can go on toward recovery with nothing holding you back.

Sometimes when you seek to express your feelings, you feel like a broken record. You become so snagged by a moment that you can't move on. If you continue over an extended period of time to keep going over and over the same feelings and don't seem to be able to get out of the groove and find some resolution to your feelings, we encourage you to seek some professional help so that you can move on. Your minister is a good person to give you some direction as to where you can get help and counsel.

Guilt over the Circumstances of Death

"But I Was Responsible!"

"I made the decision to end her life. The doctors said she was holding on only because of the machines. The machines were keeping her alive. The doctors said there was nothing else that they could do. So I made the decison. But there is still a nagging doubt in my mind. Maybe she would have come around. Maybe God would have worked a miracle. Maybe I shouldn't have made the choice."

Similar situations become more and more frequent with our new technology. We make decisions based on the limited knowledge we have available. But we never know for sure, nor can we. If we had all the information, if we were God . . . but we did the best that we could do. These are difficult decisions! Once made, the decision needs to be committed to God. Give it up to him. Ask him to take it and then let it go! Leave it with God and don't take it back or keep judging and rejudging. Ultimately God will be the judge, and you will find God to be a more loving, understanding, and compassionate judge of you than you are of yourself.

"I caused the accident; I was responsible," says the man who crashed the car in which his wife was killed. "I held the gun that went off," says the boy who accidentally shot his friend. The mother who one time, just once, didn't look behind the car when she backed out of the drive mourns, "It was my fault!" Such painful words! Such anguish! Such guilt! There are those times when someone is actually responsible for the death of another.

Perhaps you pronounce yourself guilty, or the courts do, or maybe the mass media sentence you. In the final analysis the result isn't much different. There seems to be no way to forgive yourself, let alone find anyone else's forgiveness. It may also seem that there is no way that God could forgive you. The way seems so dark that you wonder if you can ever make it through.

This is a most difficult valley of grief to get through. You can't walk it alone! You need to walk through it hand in hand with Christ. You need the help, guidance, and support of others. It is important in these circumstances to seek guidance from a trained and trusted counselor. The human psyche is complex. It's not easy to understand our motivation or how and why we make the decisions we do, especially decisions which turn out, in our estimation, to be wrong. A counselor can help you as you work your way through this complicated valley of grief with all of its twists and turns.

In biblical terms, to miss the mark or standard that God has set for us is sin. We all sin, and in God's eyes sin is sin. As God looks at sin, there are no big and little sins. If you miss, you miss. And the Bible tells us that we all miss; we all sin. In God's eyes you are no better or worse than the next guy. God stands ready to reach out and forgive you! Even more remarkable is that God will never remember your mistake or hold it against you! God's radical, total, complete forgiveness is available for the asking. An essential step is to ask for that forgiveness. Until you've done this, you'll find it difficult, if not impossible, to forgive yourself.

In a vertical dimension, as God looks on humankind, sin is sin. But on a horizontal plane, as person relates to person, not all sin is the same or bears the same consequences. On the human plane the taking of another life—accidentally, negligently, or even intentionally—is devastating. Sin, although forgiven by God, may leave scars which are forever with you. And the scars of having been responsible for another's death are most painful to bear.

To punish yourself continually will not bring back the person who is gone. To let your guilt fester and eat away at your insides not only cannot bring back the one who has gone but will also compound the tragedy by destroying you. Then two lives, not one, will be lost; and that doesn't make sense.

The great Good News of the Bible is that through Jesus Christ you can have a new beginning. You may wish with all your heart that what happened had not happened and that you could start over. The great Good News is that the past can be forgiven and that Christ can give you a new beginning. The Bible says, "Therefore, if any one is in Christ, he is a new creation; the old has passed away, behold, the new has come" (2 Corinthians 5:17). When you discover that new life, you can begin, slowly, to learn to forgive your past as God has forgiven you and to take the first, halting steps of a new life. God *does* love you and have a wonderful plan for your life, and it's a plan for your good. Yes, the scars will remain, but, as you may have noticed, the people who bear the scars are usually more conscious of them than are others.

How to Let Healing Happen

If you have been responsible for another's death, we suggest these steps toward healing:

1. *Accept* that what has happened has happened. You cannot, no matter how much you wish, turn back the hands of time. If you were to blame, accept the blame. If it was an accident, accept that it *was* an accident. If it was a decision to remove the machines or not to seek further treatment, accept that a decision had to be made and that you made the best decision you could.

2. *Confess* your share of any blame. First confess to God and then confess to another person. (For legal reasons you may want to make your confession to a minister. In most states ministers and lawyers have "privileged communication" status and cannot be forced to divulge information disclosed to them.)

3. *Mourn* the death of the person involved and the incident.

4. *Allow* yourself to be forgiven by God, and allow yourself to forgive yourself.

5. *Let go* of the person who is gone, of the incident, and of your involvement in the incident. You may want to create a symbolic moment of "letting go."

6. *Determine* that some good is going to come out of this terrible experience, not in the sense of making atonement (since you have already been forgiven!), but in the sense of choosing to find the good in a bad situation.

7. *Find* a counselor who can help you not only through this process but also in moving on with your life.

Ways to Deal with Guilt

You can either hold on to your guilt or let it go.

Living with Guilt

You can choose to live with your guilt. If you feel that you need to punish yourself for what has happened; or you feel unworthy of being loved, especially by the one who has died; or you feel that *you* must atone for your guilt; or if you are withdrawing from others and rejecting their help; then you are making the choice that you will walk into the valley and set up housekeeping at the bottom. You may say, "There is no choice. This is the way it has to be." Your pain and suffering do not allow you to judge clearly. You're going through grief work and you need somone to go through the valley with you. This is not the time to make decisions about what the rest of your life will be like.

It's hard to ask for forgiveness and even harder to forgive yourself. It's easy to think, "If I do this penance, I will even the score and repay my debt." While you may begin with good intentions, by the time you reach your original penance goal, you will have raised the limits. When you act as your own judge and pronounce your own sentence, you're assuring yourself that there will never be an end. You'll never get on with your life because you'll always be paying your debt!

Being Forgiven

Guilt doesn't resolve itself; it doesn't just go away. It has to be dealt with. It is not easy to do this. Where there is guilt, it must be taken care of. Theologically, the word for taking care of guilt is "atonement." It means that someone has paid the price for your sin, your shortcomings, and has taken to himself the burden of your guilt. Atonement isn't cheap! If it were, God would never have sent his Son to atone for your sins and to take to himself the burden of our guilt. God knew that guilt wouldn't just go away, that it couldn't be swept under the rug. And so God sent Christ to atone for us!

In the final analysis guilt needs to be confessed. Confess your guilt, ask forgiveness from other parties if necessary, but especially ask forgiveness from God. In the depths of divine forgiveness you'll be able to forgive yourself. God has a plan for our lives. That plan is for us to be happy and productive and loving. But that plan sometimes gets messed up. We get in our own way and in God's way. God sees that we can't get out of our predicaments ourselves and so steps in and says, "There are some things that are just too big for you to handle; so I've done it myself. I've done it for you."

God knows that often we can't make things right. But God also recognizes that things need to be made right. God steps in to do just that! Paul says, "While we were yet sinners Christ died for us" (Romans 5:8). This is God's gift to us, no strings attached. God gave us this gift in the middle of all our difficulties—while we were still in the valley. All we have to do is take it. His sacrifice opened the way between God and humankind, restored our relationship, and made for peace and new life.

Confess your guilt. Let it go! You will feel release! You will feel that you can go on! It will restore the relationship between you and God. It can restore your relationship with others and even your relationship with yourself.

Questions for Growth and Discussion

1. What are your should-haves?

2. In your own words write a note to God asking to be forgiven for all your should-haves and asking God to lift your guilt and release you from it!

Today's date:_____

5

The Best Is Yet to Come

There is nothing wrong with Christians grieving; in fact there's a good deal right with it! Paul writes, "Brothers, we do not want you to be ignorant about those who fall asleep, or to grieve like the rest of men, who have no hope" (1 Thessalonians 4:13, NIV). This has sometimes been interpreted to mean that Christians shouldn't grieve. This mistaken interpretation has encouraged some Christians to attempt to avoid grief work or to feel guilty about their grief. Paul is *not* saying that we should not grieve. He *is* saying that Christians should grieve, but not as those who have no hope. He is rejoicing in the midst of grief in the victory that Christ has already won. Those who have died, according to Paul, have fallen asleep in Christ and they will awake with him. Paul continues with the tremendous affirmation, "We believe that Jesus died and rose again and so we believe that God will bring with Jesus those who have fallen asleep in him" (1 Thessalonians 4:14, NIV).

The Biblical Meaning of Grief

Jesus said in the Sermon on the Mount, "Blessed are those who mourn, for they will be comforted" (Matthew 5:4, NIV). The word "mourn" here refers to passionate grief which is expressive and emotional. In the Hebrew tradition grief was freely expressed. Death was a more familiar part of family experience when families lived together under one roof, infant mortality rates were high, and few people lived to old age. Hebrew grief was very elaborate and at times bordered on hysteria. Professional mourners composed poems the lengths of which were directly related to the deceased persons' importance.

In the Old Testament twenty-six different Hebrew words are used for "grieve" and "grief." The variety of words and their meanings indicates that the Hebrews understood the wide range of emotions in grief. In the Old Testament *grief* means to labor, suffer, vex, enrage, torment, embitter, harass, agitate; to be weary, tired, depressed, dejected, heavy, vehement, wretched, angry—and the list goes on! The Hebrew people used many words to flesh out the meaning of the process we call grief. The writers of the Bible understood what a grieving person goes through! There was no stoic tradition of hiding grief and no encouragement to "be strong" but, rather, a rich tradition of expressing and working through grief.

Jesus Wept

One of the most beautiful accounts in the Bible is when Jesus arrived at the home of Mary, Martha, and Lazarus after Lazarus had died. Jesus shared fully in their grief while knowing all along that he would call Lazarus back to life.

> When Jesus saw her weeping, and the Jews who had come along with her also weeping, he was deeply moved in spirit and troubled. "Where have you laid him?" he asked.
> "Come and see, Lord," they replied.
> Jesus wept.
> Then the Jews said, "See, how he loved him!" . . .
> Jesus, once more deeply moved, came to the tomb . . . (John 11:33-38, NIV).

After praying, Jesus then called Lazarus back to life and out of the tomb.

If you study the Greek words, you discover that the rest of the folks were weeping without hope, bitterly bewailing the death of Lazarus. But the other word used for Jesus' weeping implies that Jesus, while sharing fully in the grief, was shedding tears of empathy and sympathy, grieving *with* the family rather than grieving *for* his friend Lazarus, whom he would raise from the dead.

The Bible tells us that on this occasion Jesus was "deeply moved in the spirit," or that he "groaned in the spirit." Examining this passage, we find that the Greek word used here carries with it a sense of anger and displeasure. Was Jesus' anger directed at Lazarus or his death? This assumption is unlikely since Jesus is "Lord of both the dead and the living." Did the Lord feel indignation with the mourning Jews, knowing that they would soon become his accusers? This, too, is unlikely, given the victorious tone of the passage. Was Jesus unhappy with his friends for their unbelief and/or reaction of grief? This is also unlikely, given his close relationship with Mary and Martha and his compassionate attitude.

This account has puzzled some, but Bible scholars believe the emotion of anger here was stirred by the sight of sorrow as sorrow. Jesus, whom the Bible tells us is one with God and was present with God at creation, realized that it was God's intention that humankind should live forever. Rebellion brought death. And Jesus was indignant at the momentary triumph of sin and the devil as evidenced in human death. He was angered at the ability of death to defeat life and grieve his beloved friends.

At the same time Christ knew the purpose for which he came to earth. He knew that he would suffer the pain of the crucifixion in order to pay the price of human sin. He knew that he would die and defeat death by rising again in order that someday not only Lazarus but also all who believe in Christ will be resurrected to live with him forever.

The Resurrection Miracle

The resurrection of Christ is the touchstone of the Christian faith. Paul says,

> If Christ has not been raised, then our preaching is in vain and your faith is in vain. . . . If Christ has not been raised, your faith is futile and you are still in your sins. Then those also who have fallen asleep in Christ have perished. If for this life only we have hoped in Christ, we are of all men most to be pitied (1 Corinthians 15:14-19).

The New Testament records a number of resurrections from the dead. Jesus raised the daughter of Jairus, Lazarus, and the son of the widow of Nain. Peter raised Tabitha (or Dorcas) at Joppa. At the time of Christ's crucifixion, Matthew reported, "The tombs also were opened, and many bodies of the saints who had fallen asleep were raised, and coming out of the tombs after his resurrection they went into the holy city and appeared to many" (Matthew 27:52-53). Hebrews' recounting of the heroes of faith tells us that "women received their dead by resurrection" (Hebrews 11:35). But the resurrection of Jesus is unique and stands in a category all by itself. Jesus, who was dead, buried, and in Sheol (or the lower regions of the earth) for three days, was physically, bodily, resurrected from the dead by the power of God. It is this resurrection that the Bible points to as the touchstone of our faith. *It is this resurrection that offers hope both in this world and in the world to come.*

In the power of his Godhead Christ overcame death and the grave and was resurrected triumphant and victorious. Jesus predicted his death and resurrection to his disciples. He gently chided them for doubting his word. And he called Thomas to inspect his wounds and verify that he was actually physically alive. The resurrection is historical fact. The Greek words used for the resurrection of Christ from the dead are different from the words used for all the other resurrections described in the New Testament.

The Resurrection Meaning

What is the meaning of the resurrection of Christ for me? How does it touch my life? How does it give me hope in the midst of my grief?

We want to suggest that the resurrection offers hope and meaning to those who are grieving in three ways:

1. Jesus is who he says he is.
2. In Christ we are raised to a new life.
3. In Christ we are destined for eternal life.

Jesus Is Who He Says He Is

Throughout his brief ministry Jesus made extravagant claims about himself. He announced, "I and the Father are one" (John 10:30). He prayed, ". . . that they may all be one; even as thou, Father, art in me, and I in thee . . ." (John 17:21). He taught his disciples that he would conquer death. He announced to the stunned Jews after he had driven the money changers out of the temple, "Destroy this temple, and in three days I will raise it up" (John 2:19). Parenthetically, John adds, "But he spoke of the temple of his body. When therefore he was raised from the dead, his disciples remembered that he had said this; and they believed the scripture and the word which Jesus had spoken" (John 2:21-22).

Jesus' credibility was inextricably linked to the promise of his own resurrection. Not only did he promise that he himself would be resurrected, but he also promised that in him others would share in his resurrection. Jesus said to Martha at the time of Lazarus's death, "I am the resurrection and the life; he who believes in me, though he die, yet shall he live, and whoever lives and believes in me shall never die" (John 11:25-26).

Jesus either was who he claimed to be or he was a con artist or an emotionally disturbed man with delusions of grandeur. The resurrection authenticated Jesus as who he claimed to be: none other than God in human form. Paul tells us in Romans that Christ was ". . . designated Son of God in power according to the Spirit of

holiness by his resurrection from the dead, Jesus Christ our Lord
. . ." (Romans 1:4).

We Are Raised to New Life

In Christ we are raised to new life. It is here that we experience the
greatest impact of the resurrection. Paul writes to the Romans.

> Do you not know that all of us who have been baptized into Christ
> Jesus were baptized into his death? We were buried therefore with him
> by baptism into death, so that as Christ was raised from the dead by
> the glory of the Father, we too might walk in newness of life.
> For if we have been united with him in a death like his, we shall
> certainly be united with him in a resurrection like his (Romans 6:3-5).

According to Paul, we share in both Christ's death and resurrection. It is in the power of Christ's resurrection that we are lifted to
a new life. Paul declares, "Therefore, if any one is in Christ, he is a
new creation; the old has passed away, behold, the new has come"
(2 Corinthians 5:17). Lifted to a new life through the resurrection,
we are called to a new life-style. "You are living a brand new kind
of life that is continually learning more and more of what is right,
and trying constantly to be more and more like Christ who created
this new life within you" (Colossians 3:10, *The Living Bible*).

We Are Destined for Eternal Life

In Christ we are destined for eternal life. The word used for eternal
or everlasting life in the New Testament means "life without end."
Jesus said, "I tell you the truth, he who believes has everlasting life"
(John 6:47, NIV). He told Nicodemus, "For God so loved the world
that he gave his only Son, that whoever believes in him should not
perish but have eternal life" (John 3:16).

Often eternal life is viewed as something off in the future, after
death, or after the resurrection. But John is clear in asserting that
eternal life is the present reality one receives when he or she believes.
"He who believes in the Son has eternal life . . ." (John 3:36a). The
life one gains in Christ is a new life that is eternal. Jesus said, "I am
the resurrection and the life; he who believes in me, though he die,
yet shall he live, and whoever lives and believes in me shall never
die" (John 11:25-26).

The life available in Christ is a life that begins at the moment of
rebirth and continues beyond the grave. It is both a present reality
and a future hope. Jesus said, "For my Father's will is that everyone
who looks to the Son and believes in him shall have eternal life, and

I will raise him up at the last day" (John 6:40, NIV). Inherent in Christ's resurrection is the promise of the resurrection of those who believe in him, a resurrection in this life to newness of life, and a resurrection after this life to a life in the presence of God forever. It is in this context that Jesus promised that he was going to prepare a place for us (John 14:1-9). Jesus prays in Gethsemane, "Now this is eternal life: that men may know you, the only true God, and Jesus Christ, whom you have sent" (John 17:3, NIV).

The Best Is Yet to Come!

Paul said, "If for this life only we have hoped in Christ, we are of all men most to be pitied" (1 Corinthians 15:19). Christ gives us hope in this life and in the life to come. Christ gives us hope in the midst of our grief. In Christ we are resurrected to a new life; this gives the person who is grieving hope for this life and the life to come. In Christ our Good Fridays can become Easter mornings and new opportunities for growth and life. In Christ we can come to terms with our own mortality and his promise of life beyond the grave, which is our resurrection hope. In Christ there is the ultimate hope of a new eon in which there will be no death and no grief. "He will wipe every tear from their eyes. There will be no more death or mourning or crying or pain, for the old order of things has passed away" (Revelation 21:4, NIV). Burned, disfigured, mangled, broken, worn-out bodies will be resurrected and made new like Christ's glorious body! This is both the reality and the hope in which Christians live. It is for this reason that we can say with Paul,

> "Brothers, we do not want you to be ignorant about those who fall asleep, or to grieve like the rest of men, who have no hope. We believe that Jesus died and rose again and so we believe that God will bring with Jesus those who have fallen asleep in him" (1 Thessalonians 4:13-14, NIV).

Question for Growth and Discussion

What personal hope do you find in the promise of the resurrection?

Today's date:_____

6

What's Normal and Abnormal in Grief

M y whole world is falling apart! Nothing's the same. I can't eat, I can't sleep, and I think I'm losing my mind. I forget where I put things. I do something, then go back and do it again. What's happening to me?"

Most people who are grieving go through similar turmoil. The loss of your loved one has totally changed your life and nothing is the same, nor will it ever be the same. Your lives touched in a beautiful way that has profoundly influenced you forever. After a while things will seem more "normal," but they will never be the same.

Much of what is normal behavior in grief goes contrary to what is generally thought of as normal, good, adjustive behavior. What would normally seem abnormal is perfectly normal in grief! There is no right or wrong way to grieve. What is right for you is what helps you to work through your grief. But because the normal behavior of grief is so different from what is usually considered normal, it's not unusual for grieving people to be very concerned about their behavior and to wonder if they are "losing their minds." This adds to the pressure! Not only are you suffering from the loss of your loved one, but you are also suffering the additional anxiety of not understanding your own confusing behavior. Family and friends are of little help because they don't understand it either.

"What's Happening to Me?"

Many questions and reactions come in a time of grief.

"Do I Need Professional Help?"

Probably not. Most of the things you're concerned about more than likely are part of the normal grief process, even though they may seen abnormal to you. In this chapter we'll discuss some of the normal aspects of grief. We hope that this will reassure you that what you're going through is perfectly normal. But if you're not sure, if you still have concerns, and if *you* want to, then we encourage you to seek some help. You might try your pastor, a counselor, or your family doctor. They can help you evaluate your feelings and behavior and will likely reassure you that what you're going through is perfectly normal in grief.

Crying

Crying is the most common, normal part of the grieving process. Many of us as children were taught not to cry, not even when crying was appropriate. Men particularly, at least in the past, were raised to believe that it was a sign of weakness to cry: "Boys don't cry." But during our grief the body produces certain involuntary reactions, including crying. Sometimes the tears will come without reason. Sometimes it seems almost impossible to stop crying. And this is a normal part of grief.

A successful professional man whose wife was murdered complained that he would be in the middle of a meeting, discussing business, not even thinking about his wife, and a color would catch his eye. Perhaps it unconsciously reminded him of the color of his wife's favorite dress, or of a sunset they enjoyed together. Or he'd hear a siren in the street, and he'd start to cry. He couldn't understand it and he couldn't control it. For this businessman, who was used to being in control, being unable to control his own feelings and emotions was one of the most frightening parts of his grief.

Often friends and relatives discourage you from crying. It's a mistake to listen to them! You need to let the tears flow when they want to. Pat told us how she was raking leaves, a task formerly done by her husband, and she was "having a good cry." A neighbor came over and said, "You shouldn't be crying. Come on now, snap out of it!" Even though this neighbor had been helpful in many ways, Pat replied in a very nice, but assertive way, "No. I *need* to cry. It's part of my healing."

The appropriateness of tears is influenced by culture. In some parts of the world you're expected to cry—the more the better! In some cultures professional mourners are hired to facilitate and encourage tears. Within our own country the appropriateness of tears varies. As we mentioned, for years men were taught not to cry. So they bottled up their emotions and died earlier than women. Fortunately, that's changing. But the appropriateness of tears for men varies from generation to generation. Dick pastored a black church in the South Bronx of New York City for six years and had many funerals, particularly for young people. It was expected that grief would be very demonstrative. Volunteer "nurses" in white uniforms stood by the family fanning them and administering smelling salts. Many times people were carried out of the funeral near hysteria. And it all was a culturally appropriate expression of grief.

In other cultures in our country, grief is expected to be very subdued. The widow who displays no emotion is encouraged and admired. People say, "How strong you were!" In our minds we have this image of Jackie Kennedy, at the funeral of her husband, President Kennedy—strong, stoic, controlled. Yet none of us can know the depth of her grief, nor can we judge her grief or anybody else's grief.

You need to let your grief flow and express itself in the way it will. Don't allow others, your culture, Jackie Kennedy, your grandmother, or anyone else to define what is normal. Each grieving person is different, and each grieving process is different. What is normal for someone else isn't necessarily normal for you. Grief is one area in which you need to do your own thing and not worry about what people think.

While trying not to hold back your tears, you don't want to force them either. Your tears will come when the time is right. Mary Brite, in her book *Triumph over Tears,* tells about her struggle with crying.

> I didn't cry for five months. I wasn't covering up; I just felt like a block of ice. I was certain that when I thawed out, I would melt away and there would be nothing left of me at all. At first I didn't feel enough to cry. I was just numb.
> Then I decided I wouldn't cry because I thought my four children would think I was adjusting and accepting death better if they didn't see tears from me. Finally, when I thought it would be a relief to cry, I couldn't.[1]

Eventually, in her own good time, Mary Brite did cry. Even if you can't cry now, eventually, when the time is right, you will.

"I Can't Sleep"

The shock of bereavement is so intense that your body reacts involuntarily in primitive and protective ways. People in grief experience a wide range of physical symptoms. You may have experienced all or some of these: dizziness, muscular pain, weakness, exhaustion, restlessness, gastrointestinal disorders, or menstrual irregularity. All of these are common.

[1] Mary Brite, *Triumph over Tears* (Nashville: Thomas Nelson, Inc., 1979), p. 73.

Insomnia is the most common physical complaint of grieving persons. Even though understanding some of the causes of this problem won't put you to sleep, you may find it helpful to understand why you can't sleep. The person you loved, particularly If It was your spouse, was a part of you. Your identity was tied up in the existence of the person who is gone. When a loved one dies, people usually feel "as though a part of me has been ripped away." That's understandable because a part of you *has* been ripped away. Your body goes on the defensive to protect against further loss. In order to sleep, you must feel a certain amount of trust, because while you are sleeping, you are most vulnerable. When you have lost a loved one, you feel assaulted. Part of you has been torn away, and you no longer feel in control. If you were to go to sleep, your body would have even less control and be even more vulnerable. So your body responds by saying, "No! I won't go to sleep! I won't risk further loss! I won't risk losing control!"

In time you will be able to sleep again. But because grief is such hard work, so demanding, so energy consuming, you need to be able to sleep now to have the strength to get through your grief. Talk to your family physician. Often he can give you something temporarily to help you sleep during this period.

Seeking Relaxation Through Meditation

We've found that many people in grief are so uptight that they are stretched taut. We've discovered that they can learn to relax by doing some simple relaxation exercises and by meditating on a comforting passage or thought. This isn't any kind of strange, cult ritual. It's just a simple relaxation exercise in which you focus on some basic spiritual concepts. We've found that this exercise can sometimes help. We use it in our seminar, and people frequently say that for the first time in their grief experience they were able to relax and rest.

Before you do this, you'll need to take the phone off the hook. Find some soothing, relaxing music that you like. Preferably something classical, perhaps Bach. Turn on the record player softly. Dim the lights. Sit in a comfortable but firm chair. Close your eyes and listen to the music. Allow it to enter into your body. Rest your hands on your thighs, palms up. Allow your head to relax, your jaw to relax, your chin to droop if it will. Become aware of the air at your fingertips. As you listen to the music, visualize the tension slowly draining from your body. You feel more and more relaxed. Various images can be used to help you. You might want to imagine that you are a melting ice cube. (Come on! If it helps, who cares if it sounds corny?) Or imagine you're milk pouring from a pitcher onto a table. As the milk spreads out across the table, you feel your tension spreading out, draining away. And you feel more and more relaxed.

You can focus on various meditation images. Try reading a particularly comforting passage of Scripture, perhaps from the Psalms. Read it in an old, familiar version and then in a new, unfamiliar version. Perhaps the new translation of the old passage will open new vistas and give new insight.

In most Christian bookstores you can find portions of the Bible on cassette recordings. Putting on your soft music and listening to the words of Scripture as you listen to the music in your relaxed state can be very helpful. You will find the combination reassuring, comforting, and relaxing. We listen differently than we read. Many of us have learned to read rapidly, which is great most of the time. But sometimes it helps to *listen* to Scripture, and listening to it gives a different dimension to the meaning of the words. We can "hear" insights that escape us when we read.

Seeking Prayer Power

Many times in the initial stages of grief, it's hard to pray. You want to commune with God, but the words just aren't there; they won't come. You should not be disturbed by this. Many great Christians have experienced this at times in their lives. But sometimes the communication can be powerful, reassuring, and comforting *without any words.* In your relaxed, meditative state you can visualize yourself in the presence of God. You can feel that divine presence in your life. You can *listen.* Too often in our communication with God we do all the talking! Sometimes it's good just to listen.

One of the greatest comforts to a person who is grieving is just to have someone "be with" him or her. In prayer, even prayer without any words or conscious thoughts, you can "be with" God!

Jeannette said,

> When I've needed to be comforted, uplifted, and blessed, it has been wonderful to communicate with God. He's always been there to comfort and strengthen me. Prayer has brought me peace and release. It's also brought me assurance that I'm with those I love and that all we've shared with one another can never be taken away.

In your communication with God you may want to imagine that

you are walking along and in the distance you see two people approaching you. They are talking together. The first one is Jesus, and the other is the person who has died, the one for whom you grieve. Speak to them. Tell both of them, one by one or together, what you have always wanted to say and perhaps were afraid to say. Then listen.

This particular meditation image can be a powerful tool in your healing! We've used this image in our seminar, and many participants have told us that this was one of the first times they felt able to relax. They were able to verbalize those things that they would like to have said to their loved one before he or she died, all those things that they never had the opportunity to say. It was a time to ask for forgiveness and understanding for all the should-haves that all grieving people have. It was a time to feel the reassurance and love of God and their loved one.

You will find these exercises particularly helpful If you do them before you go to bed. As you lie in bed, try this kind of prayer communication with God, whether verbal or nonverbal. And don't worry if you fall asleep while talking with God! What more wonderful way to fall asleep than in the arms of your heavenly Father!

"Everything Tastes Like Sand"

Along with all the changes that accompany your grief, many people report that food is tasteless, that they have no appetite, or that food "tastes like sand." Some lose weight while others seek a kind of solace in eating constantly. The funeral custom of bringing food to the home is based on a primitive idea that somehow food can compensate for loss. Some grieving persons seek to compensate by eating constantly. One said, "I've gained twenty pounds. I'm not hungry, but I eat constantly."

Changes in eating habits are normal in grief. But it's important to realize that your body is undergoing a lot of stress from the demands of your grief work. Because you need your energy, you need to eat balanced, nourishing meals even if you don't feel like it. This may be hard if you did all the cooking; you may not feel like cooking anymore. After all, without your spouse, what's the use? But for your own healing it's important that you eat good, regular meals—even if they're consumed without enthusiasm—and that you get lots of essential vitamins.

Identification

There are various ways in which you identify unconsciously with the loved one who is gone. Your spouse may have watched the same game show every evening, and you may have detested the program. But now, curiously enough, you find yourself drawn to the television and that game show. It's a way of reaching out for the person who is lost and trying to identify with him or her. You might find yourself taking up a hobby that your husband or wife liked.

Walt told us, "My wife pampered and cared for violets. I never bothered with the things before; but after she died, I just couldn't let them die. It keeps me going to care for them and figure out how to do it."

Once when Dick was on a cruise ship, he met one of the giants of American industry, whose name is on a half dozen products in our kitchen cupboard. This man's wife had died, and he had decided to take a cruise. He spent most of the cruise sitting in a deck chair, painfully struggling with the needlepoint chair cover his wife had been working on at the time of her death. This man may have been a great businessman, but he was a novice at needlepoint. He was all thumbs! But he kept struggling. It was an important part of his grief work. He was seeking to identify with his spouse and to work through his feelings of grief.

Now the ways in which you identify with your spouse may be different, but going through this process is a normal part of grief. It's not unusual for grieving persons to feel cold, which is a way of identifying unconsciously with the death of their loved one. Many times grieving people become preoccupied with their own physical health and magnify symptoms they might otherwise ignore. All of this is normal during the period of your grief recovery. It's not unusual to feel symptoms similar to the ones felt by the person who died. If your spouse had a heart attack, it's not unusual for you to feel chest pain. Don't hesitate to talk to your family doctor about symptoms you don't understand. But be assured that all this is very normal during grief recovery. If, however, after a long period of time, you find yourself obsessed with doing what your loved one did and you feel that you are carrying this identification to an extreme, then you might want to consider discussing the matter with a trained counselor.

You Are Very Vulnerable

If you've undergone major surgery, the doctors are very careful to keep the wound clean while it heals. After major surgery your body is most susceptible to infection. The loss of your loved one is a major emotional wound. Like the physical wound, it takes time to heal, and during this time of healing, you are very vulnerable. You are vulnerable emotionally; and because of the important links between your emotions and your body, you are also vulnerable physically.

London psychiatrist C. Murray Parkes has conducted extensive studies with widows and widowers and has proved conclusively a close relationship between grief and physical illness. A Parkes study of widowers showed that their death rate during the first six months of bereavement was 40 percent higher than the expected rate for married men of the same age. At one time "broken heart" was frequently listed on death certificates as the cause of death for widowed persons. Modern research indicates that this diagnosis may not have been far off.

Other studies have indicated that there exists a relationship between grief and mental illness, and there is a higher frequency of suicide among bereaved persons than among the population as a whole. There are more accidents—more broken hips, sprained ankles, and even more automobile accidents—among bereaved persons than among the population as a whole.

This is not intended to alarm you! There is considerable evidence that the persons who have the most physical and mental problems and complications are those who have not understood the grief process and who have resisted going through it. (If you're reading this book, then you're interested in the process and in what's happening to you.) We make these points to highlight the importance of realizing that you're probably more vulnerable right now than you've ever been in your life.

Don't hesitate to consult your family physician, an important resource for your healing. If you think he or she doesn't understand your needs, or if you feel brushed off or overmedicated, then find another doctor or try to explain to and educate your own doctor. Give him or her a copy of this book; it will help the doctor and other patients. But you do need a doctor to be able to discuss physical symptoms you don't understand.

Thoughts of Suicide

The pain of their loss is so great that many bereaved persons think about suicide. Suicide seems a way of "joining" the one who is gone. Now that doesn't make rational sense, but let's face it—bereavement isn't a rational time of life. Feelings *are,* as we've said before, and they're not always rational. People feel, *I just can't go on,* and that feeling is normal. It is also normal to have occasional thoughts about suicide. The bereaved person's thoughts about suicide are usually more because the person wants to escape the pain than because he or she wants to leave life. But these thoughts can cause great anxiety.

Most normal, well-adjusted people at some time think about suicide. But there is a difference between occasionally thinking about it and actually contemplating suicide, considering how you might do it and making actual preparations to take your own life. If the fleeting thought has crossed your mind that suicide might be a way out of your pain, that is normal and should not cause you anxiety. But if you are contemplating suicide as a viable alternative or are obsessed with thoughts of suicide, then you urgently need to seek some professional help.

If you're concerned that you might be suicidal, or if you're considering suicide, you should know that there is help available, help by people who will listen and not judge. The pain will not always be this intense! Life will never be the same again, but it can be good. Your family physician or pastor can direct you to people who can help.

Relief

Some people feel a sense of relief after the death of a loved one. This is especially true when you've had to watch someone you love suffer through a debilitating illness. A unique aspect of love is that you don't want the person you love to suffer. Love can be so powerful as to motivate you to take your loved one's suffering to yourself, if you could. And that follows the example of Christ's love! So if you feel a sense of relief at the death of your loved one, you needn't feel guilty or think that you're unique.

On the other hand, if you felt no such thing, don't worry. Your grief is yours alone. One woman whose husband had suffered a stroke and been hospitalized for many months remembers, "One friend told me after Harold died, 'It's lucky for you that he is gone because he was such a burden.' That hurt me deeply and she later apologized. Four years later she lost her husband, and then she understood."

"If It Weren't for the Kids and the Dog, I Probably Wouldn't Get Up"

It's not unusual for previously highly motivated, capable, active, alert people to find themselves suddenly feeling "suspended" and aimless. There seems no longer to be any purpose or meaning. You find it almost impossible to organize your day or get anything done. You start off well. You have a list of what you want to accomplish and all sorts of good intentions. What worked before in getting you organized doesn't seem to work any longer. You question your own sanity and mental stability. As Paula, a young widow in our seminar, put it, "If it weren't for the kids and the dog, I probably wouldn't get up."

Steve, an older widower, added, "Grief is not wanting to do anything. There's no longer anybody to share with."

If you went into the hospital for major surgery, you'd spend several weeks in the hospital recovering. Before you were sent home, your doctor would caution, "Take it easy for a while. Avoid any strenuous work. Get lots of rest. Eat well. Pamper yourself for a while." We all understand that major surgery creates a wound that requires lots of time to heal. We must also understand that bereavement is a major emotional wound that requires just as much time, rest, inactivity, and pampering to heal as a physical wound. In fact, it requires more! The aimlessness felt by the bereaved person is, in part, the body's way of protecting itself and providing time for emotional healing. So don't feel that you have to push yourself. Take your time. Give your body and emotions the time they need to heal. There are just some things you can't rush! It takes nine months to have a baby. Regardless of how impatient you get, it takes nine months. So it is with grief. It takes a long time—more than nine months!—and you can't rush it!

A different expression of aimlessness is seen in the way a bereaved person gets involved in a frenzy of activities, seeming to get involved for the sake of activity rather than for the purpose of the activity. If carried to an extreme, this can be a way of running away from the work of grief. But it may also be an expression of the aimlessness that's part of your own, individual way of working through your grief.

Grief work can be done on an unconscious as well as a conscious level. Just because it doesn't look on the surface as though a person is working on grief at a given moment doesn't mean that the process isn't taking place deep within.

"I Just Felt as Though I Wanted to Crawl into a Lap . . . But There Was No Lap Big Enough"

In reading through the questionnaires we gave to widowed persons in researching this book, we were struck by the frequency of two phrases: "There was nothing I could do" and "I felt helpless." Helplessness in grief has several aspects. There is a helplessness that the one you loved is gone and you are unable to do anything about your loss. And there is the helplessness of not knowing how to carry out normal tasks formerly taken care of by your spouse—things like balancing the checkbook, defrosting the refrigerator, getting the car serviced, or cooking a roast.

One of the most obvious solutions to the problem of helplessness is to become dependent on another person. But we live in a culture that places high value on independence. It's often embarrassing to be dependent on another. Our recommendation here is to take people at their word. If they say, "Call me if you need help," then by all means when you need help, make yourself call! Not only will you be helping yourself, but you'll also be doing them a favor. Often others feel a different kind of helplessness. They love you. They care. They want to help, but they don't know how. They offer, but they don't want to be pushy. When you allow them the opportunity of helping you with things that you need and want help with, you may actually be doing more for them than they do for you. Don't be afraid to let your friends help.

However, at the same time that you're letting people help, you need to be assertive. You are calling the shots! It's your life! And even if you don't feel assertive, you need to act as if you do feel assertive. Doing so will help you begin to feel a sense of control over your life and will help you start dealing with your feelings of helplessness.

Sometimes in grief you feel as if you're regressing, moving backward, perhaps to an earlier, even childish stage of life. That's also a normal part of grief, at least for a while. Shiela said, "I just felt as though I wanted to crawl into a lap, I guess my daddy's lap, but there was no lap big enough!"

Such feelings are normal in grief. But God, whose lap is always available, is there. You know the Bible says that we call God "Abba! Father!" That's an interesting phrase because in the original language it means "Daddy! Father!" And God is always there, even in the depth of our grief.

One young widow said, "I missed my husband so much and felt so alone. But I knew that God was always there 'hubbing' me, helping me through decisions that I couldn't make, husbanding me and being a father to my children."

As you move through the grief process, you will learn to cope with your feelings of helplessness, and your dependency needs will lessen. You will learn that you *can* deal with finances, you *can* fix a roast, and you *can* deal with the auto repair mechanic! With each new accomplishment you will feel just a little more self-confident.

Sensory Confusion

Initially our seminars were held in a large and very attractive memorial park. In her critique of our seminar one woman wrote, "Can't the park do something about the odor? Air deodorizer, air circulation, something! It's almost too much to bear for the person who's lost a loved one."

Our meetings were held in an attractive paneled room in a mausoleum building that was beautifully furnished with antiques, paintings, and other art objects. There was no odor except for the perfume of furniture polish, air deodorizer, and carpet shampoo. The "odor" the woman thought she smelled was the odor of death. But that was impossible because this mausoleum, like most such buildings, had two separate air systems. One system circulated air in the crypts, and the other circulated air in the rest of the building. The crypt circulation system was at a lower air pressure than the corridor air system, and both vented outside; so there was no possibility of any strange odor. The odor the woman smelled was in her head. It was not rational, but it was there and real for her nevertheless.

When Dick worked in the South Bronx, a teenager from the neighborhood died in the church van from an overdose of drugs. Dick recalls,

> We used gallons of disinfectant in that van and cans and cans of air spray. But those of us who found Leroy in the van that morning always smelled the smell. No matter how hard we cleaned and sprayed, it smelled the same. Nobody else could smell it, but we could.

Not everybody has the same reactions because the circumstances of death are different and grief reactions are different. One woman walked into her house and smelled an overpowering smell of urine. Just then the phone rang; it was the hospital informing her that her husband had died. She later found out that although he hadn't been able to get out of bed for quite sometime, just before he died he had forced himself out of bed in order to go to the bathroom. This woman had never shared this experience until she found the safety and security of our grief recovery group. She worried about this unexplainable mystery and feared she was going crazy.

Sometimes a kind of sensory confusion is normal in grief. In time, the association will fade and the confusion will lessen. But in the meantime it can be very confusing if you don't understand what's happening.

"But Isn't That Strange?"

No, not necessarily. Remember, your grief reactions are uniquely yours. The way you feel and react is normal for you. When people begin to share in our grief seminars, begin to trust us and one another, they are able to open up and share the grief reactions that they're concerned about and worry about. And they ask, "But isn't that strange?"

No, not strange at all. Not if it's part of your grief!

Sleeping in your spouse's bed or on his or her side of the bed. This is a way of feeling some kind of closeness to his or her presence in your life.

Not wanting to sleep in the same bed. Another way of reacting to the same need.

Setting an extra place even when you know he or she is not coming back. It takes awhile to adjust. Sometimes you are consciously or unconsciously resisting that adjustment.

Not wanting to clean out the closets and give away your loved one's personal things. A way of holding on a little while longer and clinging to memories.

Cleaning everything out right away. A different way of dealing with the same situation.

Dreaming about your spouse as if he or she were still alive. Even having intensely sexual dreams. These occurrences are perfectly normal. In dreams we frequently experience things as we wish they were.

Not dreaming about your spouse. If that's you, it's normal for you!

Feeling your loved one's presence in the house. Why not? Your house and your life are filled with precious memories!

Again, the bottom line is that your grief is uniquely yours. What might otherwise seem abnormal in your life at some other time is normal in grief.

Depression

Part of the essence of your grief is that you're not happy, that you feel sad and depressed. The severity of your depression depends in part on where you are in the grief process. Depression is most severe in the early stages of grief, particularly after the shock stage when you're in the suffering stage. Some depression in grief is perfectly normal. But there is another form of depression that is not always related to grief but may emerge as an abnormal expression of grief. How do you know if your feelings of depression are normal, grief depression, or are abnormal, psychological depression? Bertha Simos in her book *A Time to Grieve* presents a helpful discussion of the difference between normal depression in grief and the abnormal, pyschological dysfunction of depression.

> The normally bereaved, despite their sadness, can laugh and show a variety of emotions appropriate to environmental shifts. For example, they can laugh at the antics of an infant even in the midst of grief. Depressives remain downcast regardless of what is going on about them. The bereaved respond to reassurance, support, and comfort; depressives, if they respond at all, require urging, promises, or strong pressure. The bereaved retain the capacity for pleasure; depressives have lost the capacity to have fun. The bereaved dwell on that which was lost; depressives dwell on themselves. The bereaved may be openly angry; depressives may be irritable, critical, complaining, but open anger is missing. The bereaved feel the world is empty but realize their sense of personal emptiness is temporary; depressives feel a prolonged, intense inner emptiness. Both may have physical complaints, insomnia, and changes in sexual interest. The bereaved project a feeling of sadness in others; depressives project a feeling of helplessness, if not hopelessness.[2]

"Give Sorrow Words"

Shakespeare wrote,

> Give sorrow words: the grief that does not speak
> Whispers the o'er-fraught heart, and bids it break.[3]

[2] Bertha G. Simos, *A Time to Grieve: Loss as a Universal Human Experience* (New York: Family Service Association of America, 1979), p. 190. Reprinted from *A Time to Grieve*, by Bertha G. Simos, by permission of the publisher. Copyright 1979 by Family Service Association of America, New York.

[3] *Macbeth*, act 4, scene 3, line 209.

Shakespeare put his finger on what psychology would later dis-cover—people must work through their grief. Grief, unexpressed, leads to physical and emotional illness. Grieving is a hard and painful process. It is so painful that there is a tendency to avoid it. But flight from grief and its various manifestations offers only temporary and illusionary relief. Grief is one of those things that, if it doesn't kill you, will make you stronger.

When Is Grief Excessive?

We've already noted that much of normal grief behavior goes contrary to what is generally thought of as good, adjustive behavior. Distinguishing normal grief from abnormal grief is primarily a matter of degree. When your grief interferes with your taking care of yourself or finding any enjoyment in life; when you find yourself consistently withdrawing from life and people; when you see your personality changing and you can't control the changes; when your doctor tells you that you're sick and there is nothing physically wrong; when you suffer from unresolved guilt; and when these symptoms continue for a long period of time; then it becomes evident to you that your emotional healing is not taking place. Then you need professional help.

Dr. Beverly Mead, an Omaha psychiatrist, says, "The bereaved should be encouraged to go for professional care *any time they want to.*" The primary task in dealing with abnormal grief is to help convert it into normal grief. Often a professional person can assist you in working through your normal grief and should be consulted if you are concerned that your grief experience is taking an abnormal turn.

Questions for Growth and Discussion

1. What aspects of your grief have you not understood and have given you anxiety?

2. In the light of this chapter, can you analyze those aspects of your
   grief, understand them better, and lessen your anxiety?

Today's date: _____

7

Growing Through Grief

In time the pain will lessen, you will learn to cope, and life will go on. But will your grief be over? We don't think so. It will be easier to bear and you'll learn to live with it, but because the memory of the one who died will always be with you, we feel that you will always feel the loss. It was Sadie who said many years after her husband's death, "I still mourn for him every day." Jack told us, "I sit at the same desk and do the same job as before my wife's death. Outside I look the same, but I'm different. I am forever changed by the death of my wife."

So the grief becomes more bearable, but it's always there. Anniversaries of significant events shared with your loved one, birthdays, the anniversary of the death, and holidays all bring back past memories and pangs of sorrow. Grief recovery is a lifelong process.

Rather than look at the continuing process of grief in negative terms, we've chosen to identify a fourth and final stage of grief recovery, which we call growth. The grief continues, but less intensely, allowing this fourth and final stage to be a time of growth and discovery. We don't mean to imply that you haven't been growing through this process all along, because you have been! But we believe that identifying a fourth, final, and lifelong stage of grief recovery, the growth stage, offers the promise of light at the end of the tunnel.

This, Too, Shall Pass

An ancient Eastern potentate once asked his wise men and philosophers to come up with a single phrase that would apply to all conditions and situations in life. The king wanted always to be able to say the right thing. It was quite a challenge, but the wise men and philosophers were equal to the task. The phrase they came up with was, "This, too, shall pass."

There's a sense in which that's not such a bad attitude with which to approach the negative situations in life, including the loss of a loved one. Grief is a process, not a sentence. The most painful phase of grief, the suffering phase, will pass. But if you only adopt the attitude, "This, too, shall pass," you wish away the experience, the process, the memory, and a part of life and growth. Now that's tempting because the process is painful. But having lost a loved one, you know how precious and fragile life is and how important it is to wring from life everything it has to offer. It would be tragic to wish life away! In the negative experiences of life and even in grief there is opportunity for growth.

Going Through It Or Growing Through It

If you could choose, you'd never choose to go through this! But since you *have* to go through it, instead of just going through it, why not *grow* through it?

Growth is characteristic of all living things. Bob Dylan is supposed to have said, "A person is either being born, or he is dying." When you lose someone dear to you, it's not unusual to feel that part of you has died or even that you are slowly dying. There is a tendency to give up. Those who have lost loved ones have a significantly higher death rate than others of the same age in the general population. Yes, a part of you has died. Part of you is forever gone. That changes you! You are not the same as before and you will never again be the same. You are forever changed. And in this fact lies both the crux of the problem and your opportunity. Inherent in grief is hope—if you look for it and if you reach out and seize it. If you allow yourself to go through the process, it's possible to grow through your grief and go on.

Growth Takes Time

Like any growth process, growing through grief takes time. It doesn't happen overnight. It's hard work and it's painful, but it can also be rewarding. Gordon and Gladis DePree capture the essence of growth in this poem.

> Growing
> Is seldom a graceful process.
> It is shoots and half-formed leaves,
> Big teeth and bony knees.
> Growing is the process of something
> Becoming larger, taller,

More mature.
> And although growing
> Is not always a graceful process,
> Poised and polished and finished,
> It is preferable to its alternative . . .
For when a plant or animal or person
Or mind or spirit
Stops growing,
It begins the process of dying.[1]

You don't have to get to the fourth stage of grief recovery to grow! Whether you realize it or not, you've been growing all through the process of your grief. It's helpful and encouraging to be able to identify the elements of growth in your own life. One of the ways of doing this is through your journal. That's why we've encouraged you to keep a journal. By reading through past entries in your journal, you can see just how far you've come. Sure, you still have a long way to go, but you need to realize how far you've already come!

"How I've Grown Through My Grief"

We asked some of those who shared with us to share with you how the negative experience of their grief has become in time an opportunity for growth.

"I've done many things I wasn't sure I was able to do. I survived. I didn't fall apart. I've grown spiritually. I've seen how graciously God has softened the way as difficulties have arisen. My priorities are changing and becoming clearer. Maybe I'm bolder."

* * *

"I've realized that I'm capable of many things. I've learned to keep a positive attitude even while going through this valley."

* * *

"I've thought about myself more as an individual, discovered more who I am. I'm stronger, more independent. I have more poise. I've pursued music arranging and taken classes in which I've met interesting people."

* * *

"I am finding out that I can do things I didn't think I could. I'm also finding out that some people are worse off than I am, and I'm reaching out to them."

[1]Gordon and Gladis DePree, *The Gift* (Grand Rapids, Mich.: The Zondervan Corporation, 1976), p. 105. Taken from *The Gift* by Gordon and Gladis DePree. Copyright © 1976 by The Zondervan Corporation. Used by permission.

*   *   *

"I used to be ashamed of my feelings. But now I'm realizing that 'feelings *are*' and that everyone feels angry and sad and cries. I have grown to accept my feelings. I've also become more independent. I go out alone, which I never did before."

*   *   *

"I've planted a seed of hope. It's still painful, but as I watch it grow, I know that I am growing."

*   *   *

"I realize that I'm more capable than I thought I was. I'm becoming more of my own person. I'm trying to go on in a way that George would have been proud of."

*   *   *

When we've asked people how they've grown through their grief experience, several things have come out over and over again. You can see them in the comments above.

● People have learned to accept and deal with feelings.

● They've discovered they're a lot more capable than they ever thought!

● They've become more independent and reached out and stretched in new ways.

● They've discovered more about themselves and who they are. These are all positive rewards in personal growth. They don't happen overnight, but they can happen!

Experiencing Resurrection

Christians believe that all of life has meaning and purpose under the lordship of Christ. In order for us to distill the meaning and purpose out of our grief, it is helpful to view what we're going through in resurrection terms.

The Bible teaches resurrection in three different but intimately related senses. There is the resurrection of Christ from the dead, an accomplished fact of faith and history. There is the end-time promise of the resurrection of the dead and the gathering of believers to be with the Lord forever when Christ returns. This is a future hope based on faith and belief in the promises of Christ. There is also an existential, here-and-now resurrection which the believer experiences in this life in union with Christ. Paul says, "We were therefore buried with him through baptism into death in order that, just as Christ was raised from the dead through the glory of the Father, we too may live a new life" (Romans 6:4, NIV). Inherent in the concept of new life is the concept of growth. It is precisely because of the accomplished fact of Christ's resurrection that we can, in him, experience our own resurrection from death to life and our opportunity for growth. The concept of the resurrection thus becomes a key factor in understanding the idea of growing through our grief.

As you depend on and trust in Christ, he can resurrect you from the death you now feel in the suffering of your grief. He can lift you up to a new life and show you a new future. It won't be the same, but it can be good.

The psalmist wrote,

> Even though I walk through the valley of the shadow of death,
>   I will fear no evil, for you are with me;
>   your rod and your staff, they comfort me.
>
> —Psalm 23:4, NIV

As we mentioned at the beginning of this book, your grief experience is like walking through the valley of the shadow of death. You are going through the valley of your grief. It is a long and difficult journey, but after you've gone through the valley and come out the other side, the reward is that you are resurrected to a new life.

We might visually diagram the journey to resurrection and growth in this way:

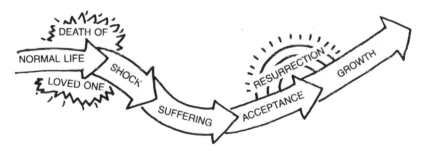

In order to go through the valley and reach the other side and experience resurrection, you must die to your former life. This means letting go. Letting go of the one who has died. Giving that person up to the Lord. Because you don't want to let go, because you want to hang on, letting go is the hardest part of your grief work. But it must be done in order for you to grow. Letting go doesn't mean blotting the other person out of your memory or forgetting all the happy experiences you shared together. Letting go means coming to the recognition that the other is gone and that you must go on alone.

Dr. Richard Krebs in the book *Alone Again* offers some very helpful insights, particularly in this area of "letting go" in order to experience resurrection. Krebs views the period of letting go as the deepest and darkest part of the valley. He says,

> Not everyone goes through the period of letting go at the same speed. . . . Some people spend more time going down into the valley. Others let go even more quickly. Some never get to the valley at all because they are afraid of what they will find there.
>
> No one really wants to let go and go down into the valley because the valley means pain and suffering. Yet the valley lies in the middle of a resurrection journey. It has to be crossed to get to the other side, the side of a full, complete single life. . . .
>
> With the concept of resurrection, Christians attempt to describe what it feels like to undergo a radical change. Moving completely, successfully, from a married to a single life is such a radical change that it can only be adequately described in terms of a dying and rising again.
> . . .
>
> As you begin to let go of your mate, you will find yourself starting your own resurrection experience. After you let go of your mate, you begin a journey which feels like sliding into a valley. The resurrection journey takes you down before you rise again. Death precedes new life.[2]

The letting-go phase really describes the suffering phase of our grief. The reason why the suffering phase is so intense is that we are suffering the agonies of letting go and moving toward acceptance of the fact that our loved one is not coming back. For one to move on, there must be a letting go. It doesn't happen in an instant; it happens gradually, although there may be a conscious moment of letting go. Pat recalled that it was while the minister was speaking of the resurrection hope in church on Easter Sunday morning that she let go of her husband and gave him up to God.

Bob's wife was killed in a plane crash in San Diego. It was the spectacular kind of crash that was captured in chilling detail by a news photographer. The photo was so spectacular that it appeared again and again. Every time he saw it, Bob was again reminded of his wife's death. Bob read and reread the F.A.A. report of the crash. After studying the report thoroughly, he came to the conclusion that

[2]Richard Krebs, *Alone Again* (Minneapolis; Augsburg Publishing House, 1978), pp. 42-43. Reprinted from *Alone Again* by Richard Krebs, copyright 1978, by permission of Augsburg Publishing House.

the disaster happened so fast that there had been little or no time for terror and that his wife and the others on the plane had been killed instantly. Researching the accident alleviated Bob's fears that his wife had suffered. In the process of working through his grief, Bob attended a grief seminar in California. It was held in the mountains, and at the conclusion of the seminar a campfire was held at night. Participants were asked to take a pine cone and place it in the fire as a way of symbolically giving up their loved one and letting go. Bob's wife had always loved pine cones, and as he dropped his pine cone into the fire and watched the embers go up into the sky, he saw a shooting star. It was Bob's way of letting go. For him the shooting star was divine assurance that his wife was with the Lord.

Your way of letting go doesn't have to be that dramatic, but it sometimes helps to have a conscious moment of letting go and of committing your loved one into God's care.

After the letting go and the acceptance comes the resurrection. Krebs asks,

> What is it like to rise? Glorious! Not as glorious as the final resurrection that will follow our physical death, but it is glorious, nevertheless.
> To begin to see some light again as you come out of the dark valley. To realize that the slant of the ground under your feet is no longer down. To sense that your feet are no longer encased in lead, but are beginning to feel light again. To feel that the load you have been carrying on your shoulders is finally being lifted. However you experience your resurrection, there is nothing quite like rising again.
> Knowing that you will experience pain in the valley, that you will have to die to your former married life, should not prevent you from taking the journey. You will feel anxious and lonely in the valley before you can begin to rise again. But since you know what to expect, you will be less frightened, less upset. Most importantly, you need to remember that the journey has a happy ending.[3]

You Don't Go It Alone

As a Christian you face the loss of a loved one with Christ at your side. You don't go through the valley alone. Your commitment to Christ in life and in death makes it possible for you to ask Christ to see you through this valley and to lift you up on the other side to new life.

Dick writes a syndicated newspaper column called "Ideas for Positive Living." One of his columns dealt with the idea of Christ being the one friend who's always there, even in the midst of your

[3] *Ibid.,* pp. 60-61.

loneliness, even when you walk through the valley. The column has been so helpful to so many people that we share it with you now.

One Essential Friend

Dr. William Glasser in his book *Reality Therapy* says, "Every man needs one essential friend." If you've got one essential friend, you've got the answer to loneliness. Everyone needs one essential friend: a friend with whom he can be open and honest and level with. Everyone needs a friend so close and trusted he can expose himself completely without feeling vulnerable. Everyone needs a friend who will always be there. "There are friends who pretend to be friends, and there is a friend who sticks closer than a brother" (Proverbs 18:24, RSV).

I have such a friend. His name is Jesus Christ! He has promised to be with me always, to never leave me, and never forsake me. He is the one essential friend. In my failure he is with me. In my success, he is beside me, having brought me there in the first place. He gives me dreams and gives me the courage to achieve those dreams. He is with me when I'm sick and when I'm in trouble. He is present in my family. He, and he alone cures the loneliness of my spirit. For it is he, and he alone, who brings me back into fellowship with the God who created me and allows me to live out God's purpose for my life!

Jesus Christ is a friend who sees me as I really am and accepts me. I don't have to play games or be phony with him. He's my friend who loves me and who would, and did, die for me.

You never need be lonely as long as you know there is one person who really loves you and cares for you and will always stick by you. Such a person is Jesus Christ. He will never leave you nor forsake you. He will be with you always to the end of time. The price of his friendship? He asks only that you make a commitment to love him—forever! And his promise to you is that he will love you forever![4]

Your Particular Passage

For the widowed person this period of change, of growth, is a "passage" from one stage of life to another. It is a movement from a married state to a single state. For those who married young and whose identity has been shaped by their spouses, it requires the establishment of new and separate identities. You may not have taken the time to establish a separate identity before marriage. Now you have both the challenge and the opportunity of going back and building a separate identity.

Gail Sheehy in her popular book *Passages* uses the illustration of a lobster, which sheds its hard, protective shell in order to grow, and applies this example to the challenge of growth in the "passages"

---

[4]Richard Lewis Detrich, *God Loves You and I Do Too* (Milwaukee: Ideals, 1978), p. 54. Used with permission.

of our lives. During the period after the shedding of the shell, the lobster is exposed and vulnerable as a new covering grows to replace the one that was lost. During the grief process, you are passing from one stage of life to another, from a married to a single state. Sheehy says, "With each passage from one stage of human growth to the next we, too, must shed a protective structure. We are left exposed and vulnerable—but also yeasty and embryonic again, capable of stretching in ways we hadn't known before."[5]

It's easy for you to identify with the feeling of being left exposed and vulnerable. But you need to understand that grief is also an opportunity to grow and appreciate the feeling of being "yeasty and embryonic."

Gail Sheehy is writing about the general passages of adult life. But her concept of adult "passages" is applicable to the grief process if you realize that you are passing from a married to a single state. She says,

> The work of adult life is not easy. As in childhood, each step presents not only new tasks of development but requires a letting go of the techniques that worked before. With each passage some magic must be given up, some cherished illusion of safety and comfortably familiar sense of self must be cast off, to allow for the greater expansion of our own distinctiveness.
>
> What I'm saying is, we must be willing to change chairs if we want to grow. There is no permanent compatibility between a chair and a person. And there is no one right chair. What is right at one stage may be restricting at another or too soft. During the passage from one stage to another, we will be between two chairs. Wobbling no doubt, but developing. . . . *Times of crisis, of disruption or constructive change, are not only predictable but desirable. They mean growth.* (Emphasis is ours.)[6]

Now certainly the loss of a loved one isn't in any sense a "constructive change." But remember, Sheehy is writing about general passages in adult life, not the experience of grief in particular. But her point is well taken and applicable to the process of grief. When you choose to wring the positive out of an otherwise negative situation, this can become a time of growth.

"I'm OK!"

To go through this loss experience, this grief process, shakes us

[5] Gail Sheehy, *Passages* (New York: E. P. Dutton, 1976), p. 20. Copyright © 1974, 1976 by Gail Sheehy. Reprinted by permission of the publisher, E. P. Dutton, Inc.
[6] *Ibid.*, p. 21.

to our bones. It's devastating. It changes all of life. It can either shake your self-confidence or build it. It can destroy your self-image or strengthen it. It's important that you know, feel, and believe that you are a significant and important person in your own right!

In our seminars we ask people to join us in making several affirmations by saying them out loud. We do this several times. The first attempt is usually halfhearted; many in the group aren't convinced of what they're saying. At some points they show noticeable resistance to admitting what is reality. But after a while acceptance comes. After repeated affirmation they start to believe, and they start to live the reality of their new lives.

Here are the affirmations (with some comments thrown in).

"*I am a widowed person.*" (Yes, it hurts. Whether you like the term or not, and many people don't, it is an affirmation of the reality of your situation.)

"*I'm single.*" (There's usually a lot of hesitation at this point, a lot of emotion. This is hard to say because it brings home the reality of your loss. Don't expect to be able to accept it at first, or even to say it, but keep trying. In time you will be able to make the important step of accepting that you are now alone again, a single person once more.)

"*I'm OK!*" (You really are! You may not always feel it, but you're doing a lot better at this thing called grief recovery than you would ever have thought posssible! If you're not, read on. Come back and reread this section in a few months, and you'll realize how far you've come and how much you've handled.)

"*I'm a good person!*" (This is true—whatever you've done or haven't done. Even if you've gotten angry and cursed God out loud, in his eyes you are still a good person! God paid a very dear price for you! You're his no matter what!)

"*God loves me and I do too!*" (The first part is usually easier than the second. It's because *God* loves you that *you* can love you, no matter what. You may not like all your feelings or your angry outbursts or the way you sometimes act or don't act, but you can still like you.)

"*I have a future!*" (This may not seem to be true now, but you do! We've discovered that *where individuals are* in the grief process has much to do with how they feel about the future. Those in shock don't realize that there *is* a future. Persons in the suffering stage are hurting so much that they hope and pray there isn't a future, at least not if it is anything like the present. Those in the acceptance stage have an agnostic attitude toward the future—they don't know whether there is or isn't one. But persons in the growth stage of grief sense that there is a future. It will be different, but it can be good!)

You may not care to make these affirmations now. That's OK. But dog-ear this section of the book and in two, three, or six months come back and read and reread this section. At some point the time will come when you are ready to make these positive affirmations about who you are and about your future. When that time comes, you'll know that you've made a lot of progress and come a long way!

When that time does come, we suggest that you write these affirmations down and put them in your purse or your wallet, on your desk, your mirror, the refrigerator door, or the dashboard of your car. Repeat them to yourself several times each day for two weeks. You'll find that you'll start believing them and living them.

"I AM A WIDOWED PERSON."

"I'M SINGLE."

"I'M OK!"

"I'M A GOOD PERSON!"

"GOD LOVES ME AND I DO TOO!"

"I HAVE A FUTURE!"

Questions for Growth and Discussion

1. How have you been able to grow through your grief thus far?

2. Where are you right now in your journey toward a new life?

3. What is the hardest part for you about letting go?

Today's date:_____

8

Why?

It was a sultry summer evening. A thunderstorm had swept across the mountains, and lightning was streaking over the foothills. Thunder was crashing, and hail was noisily bouncing off our cedar-shake roof. Our little girls, Noelle and Becky, jumped into bed with us at the first crash of thunder. Noelle, the theologian in the family, wanted to know, "Why does God make the thunder and the lightning?" At home Dick always defers to Nikki on such theological questions. Nikki tried an answer. Then Noelle asked, "But if God loves us, why does he let the thunder and lightning happen? Why?"

* * *

Dick received this letter from a white-haired man who attended one of our seminars.

Dear Dr. Detrich:

I want to thank you and Nikki for the time and understanding you have shown me. I will never forget the time after one of the sessions when I stood by my wife's grave and Nikki came over and talked to me. I think she is the most kind and understanding person in this world.

I wish I could get something out of my mind. You say that Jesus loves us all. I think he has an odd way of showing it. After living, working, fighting, and loving my wife for thirty-nine years, when things should slow up for us to enjoy, "Bang!" she is removed from this earth. Why?

The Haunting Question of Our Grief

Why? You ask that question over and over again. You ask your closest friends. And in your lonely moments at night you shout it at God: "*Why?* If you love me, why have you taken my loved one?" The question isn't always asked consciously because many people

95

are afraid to question God. But it's a question which needs to be asked as a part of our grief.

When Noelle was about two, in the "why" stage of life, when everything was "why" this, "why" that, she and Dick were taking a walk one evening. Noelle had bombarded Dick with every "why" in the book. "Why is the grass green? Why is the sky blue?" On and on. Finally she asked, "Daddy, why does the sun go down?" By this time Dick was close to exasperation, and he replied, "Honey, so you can go to bed and get up tomorrow and ask 'Why?' all day!" Noelle didn't appreciate that answer. She put her hands on her little two-year-old hips, turned to Dick, and said, "Dad, if I not ask why, I not know why. You know why." So, if we don't ask, we'll never know. And we *need* to know. It's part of our healing.

The Search for Meaning

We all need to see some cosmic significance and meaning in our lives and in the lives of those we love. Part of the normal grief process is the search for that meaning. We are looking for meaning in life and meaning in death; meaning in our lives and the lives of the persons we loved and meaning in their deaths. Viktor Frankl said, ". . . the striving to find a meaning in one's life is the primary motivational force in man."[1] Perhaps never before has your search for meaning been as intense as it is right now.

Don't be afraid to ask the questions. Don't be intimidated or discouraged if the answers are hard to find and long in coming or if you never find all the answers. Dr. John Piet, a friend and professor of Dick's in seminary, always said, "The important thing in life is not to have all the answers, but to ask the right questions." There are people who go through life and never know what the questions are, let alone the answers! This is a time to ask the questions!

In one of our seminars Bea blurted out, "Now that my husband is gone, who am I anyway?" She was discovering the right questions. Someone else said, "Yes, and what's the meaning of my life any-more?" Another one of the *right* questions. "Why?" is one of the right questions. It begs to be asked as part of your grief recovery.

No Easy Answers

There are no easy answers. Those who appear to have all the answers either (*a*) don't know what the questions are, (*b*) have never

[1]Viktor Frankl, *Man's Search for Meaning* (New York: Simon and Schuster, Inc., 1959), p. 154.

gone through the loss of a loved one, or (c) have arrived at their answers slowly and painfully.

Shortly after we began our grief seminars, we encountered our own grief. Nikki's dad died at age fifty-nine of heart failure. Dick had worked as an assistant with Nikki's dad for three years. That's how we met! So together we lost a man who was a father, a friend, a counselor, a mentor.

Harland Steele was a special man not only to us but to many people. He was a powerful preacher and a good counselor who'd helped many families through difficult times. He'd pastored several large churches and had been radio minister of his denomination. He had started writing and had had several articles published. In his early fifties when he was at his prime professionally, his deteriorating heart condition forced him to retire from the ministry. This was a difficult circumstance for all of us to accept, but especially for Harland. Jesus said, "The harvest is plentiful, but the laborers are few; pray therefore the Lord of the harvest to send out laborers into his harvest" (Matthew 9:37). Harland wrestled with this. He saw so much need and wondered, "If that's true, then why has God sidelined me just when I'm able to make my greatest contribution?"

Why?

There were no easy answers.

Although he had great physical limitations and knew that his time was limited, Harland threw himself into his writing and did whatever work he could in the church. At the time of his death he had a complete outline for a book that would have dealt with wrestling with the problem of human suffering. It was just an outline, but it would have been a good book because it had come out of the cauldron of his own suffering.

When he died, we had to wrestle with the looming question—why?

Looking for God's Will in the South Bronx

When Dick served a church in the South Bronx of New York City for six years, he had twenty-one funerals during that time. Only one of these was a man who died a natural death. The rest were all for kids. Kids who were shot, stabbed, thrown off buildings, had their throats slashed, or overdosed on drugs. Dick says, "Believe me, I asked why! Many times. And I still do! And I don't know why. But someday in heaven I'm going to stand face to face with the God I love and who loves me, and I'm going to ask him, 'Why?' And I expect that there will be quite a line, and quite a wait."

It was Halloween night, late. George was coming home from work. It was about 11 PM when he entered his apartment building in Patterson Housing Project in the South Bronx. The elevator wasn't working, as usual; so George bounded up the stairs to the fifth floor. Even after a day's work, at age twenty George had energy to spare. He stepped up to the door of his apartment, 5-A, and put the key in. He never opened the door. He was stabbed from behind, repeatedly. And Helen found her son in a pool of blood, dead, at her front door.

Years later I asked Helen how she managed to cope. She said, "George was the Lord's. The Lord gave him to us for a while, and then the Lord took him back. It was just the Lord's will."

That was no easy answer for Helen! She'd agonized over that—pleaded, shouted, cried, and demanded an answer. Slowly, painfully, over the years she'd arrived at that conclusion. For her it was the right answer because it was her answer.

Helen has now gone to be with her Lord. Dick says, "I would never have questioned her answer while she was alive, because it was her answer. But I've never been sure."

Dick explains, "As I understand God's will, his will is not for a young man in the prime of life to be brutally murdered. That's not God's will! Never was, never will be! It's not God's will that Leroy overdosed on methadone, or Greenie had his throat slashed, or Belinda was blown away with a shotgun blast, or José was thrown off a roof. That's not God's will!"

God's will *is* that humankind should love and enjoy God forever! God's will was that people should live forever! God created us for fellowship with him, fellowship with one another, and that was forever. But God's will was frustrated by human disobedience and rebellion. Instead of listening to God, human beings chose to listen to Satan. So evil entered into our world. The world in which we live was corrupted, distorted, perverted. It was not long before brother killed brother. In punishment for this rebellion, human beings, who were created to live forever, now face death.

We know a minister whose sixteen-year-old son was killed because another driver drank too much. The drunk driver decided to pass another car on the crest of a hill and collided head-on with our friend's son, and the boy was killed instantly. Is that God's will? We think not.

Do Things Just Happen?

If it's not God's will, do these things just happen? Do things in this world happen at random? Is God in charge or is God not in charge? You're asking the right questions!

Reverend Pat Shaughnessy was in Los Angeles International Airport when a bomb went off twenty-five feet from where he was standing. Three people were killed and Shaughnessy was one of thirty-six injured. He was not expected to live but he did, although he lost his right leg. When he was interviewed by Dr. Robert Schuller on "Hour of Power," Shaughnessy said,

> God knew the bomb was there and He knew I was there. It was not an accident. It was an incident. You see, I don't believe that accidents happen. I believe that God directs everything, and it's all for our good. God didn't hear the bomb go off and say, "Wow, what was that noise in Los Angeles?" God knew the bomb was there, and He knew I was standing there, and He was saying, "Pat, I have a wonderful, wonderful plan for you. . . . You're not going to like it at first, but trust me."[2]

God *is* in control of this world and of what happens to his children. The Bible assures us, "The Lord reigns, let the earth rejoice . . ." (Psalm 97:1). Jesus assured us, "Are not two sparrows sold for a penny? And not one of them will fall to the ground without your Father's will. But even the hairs of your head are all numbered. Fear not, therefore; you are of more value than many sparrows" (Matthew 10:29-31).

If God Is in Charge, Then Why?

If God is in charge and loves us, then why do things happen in our lives which seem to go against God's expressly stated will and purpose? Theologians have distinguished between what God wants and wills and what God allows to happen. They've called what God *allows* to happen in this world, but may not wish to happen, God's "permissive will." In other words, God does permit some things to happen that may go against his expressed will.

Look at Job. Job was a man who loved God and did God's work and God's will. But the Bible portrays Satan as challenging God. "Of course Job loves you! Look at all that you've given to him! He loves you for what's in it for him. But you take some of that away, you bring some tough times into Job's life, you give him some grief and see what happens." God refuses to do this. But in the great

[2]Robert Schuller, *Turning Your Stress into Strength* (Irvine, Calif.: Harvest House, 1978), pp. 18-19.

cosmic warfare between God and Satan, for His own purposes, God *allows* Satan to bring all kinds of grief and calamity into the life of Job as a way of putting Job to the test and proving his faith. Job loses everything that he has, including his entire family. His friends come—you may know some of them—with all of their easy answers. Job goes through it all; he goes down into the depths of the valley; he asks many difficult questions; but he comes through. He comes out on the other side, and God is with him and blesses him.

Yes, God made the world and controls it. There isn't anything that happens that God doesn't know about. But at the same time that God created human beings, he gave them the will to choose, the ability to choose evil or to choose right. God is not a grand puppeteer in the sky dangling us on strings so that when they are pulled, we move. Nor, to change the metaphor, is God a grand computer programmer who's programmed us all. God has given us the freedom to choose. Often we choose the wrong way and go against God's will. God permits it, allows it; but it brings pain and suffering. That is the painful result of rebellion and sin.

When you are in grief, much of your world seems out of control. So it is important that you decide to believe and affirm by faith—even though you may not feel it in your gut—that God *is* in control, even though it may not always seem that way.

God Has a Plan

We like the illustration of a person weaving a tapestry. From one side of the loom we see a confusing mass of color, threads, and knots. It doesn't look like much and we don't understand it. Sometimes our lives can be that way. But God sees the grand design for all of our lives. He sees our lives not only as they are but also as they will become. He sees not only this side but the other side as well.

Paul said, "We walk by faith, not by sight" (2 Corinthians 5:7). We have to believe this! Unless God is in control, nothing makes any sense! In the letter to the Hebrews, faith is defined for us. "Now faith is the assurance of things hoped for, the conviction of things not seen" (Hebrews 11:1). We believe that God *is* in control. We believe that God has a wonderful purpose and plan for our lives and the lives of the people we love. We believe that we are all held tenderly and lovingly in the hollow of God's hand.

It's summed up beautifully for us in the words of the Heidelberg Catechism. Written in German over four hundred years ago, shortly after the Reformation, the Heidelberg Catechism sought to express the basic beliefs of the Christian faith in question-and-answer form. It begins with what Viktor Frankl called the "primary motivational force in man." It begins with a search for meaning.

The Heidelberg Catechism asks the question, "What is your only comfort in life and in death?"

Listen to this answer!

> That I am not my own but belong—body and soul, in life and in death—to my faithful Savior Jesus Christ. He has fully paid for my sins with his precious blood and has set me free from the tyranny of the devil. He also watches over me in such a way that not a hair can fall from my head without the will of my heavenly Father. In fact, all things must work together for my salvation. Because I belong to him, Christ by his Holy Spirit assures me of eternal life and makes me whole-heartedly willing and ready from now on to live for him.[3]

Even if you don't have all the answers, that's enough to let your heart sing!

Eternal Truth

We are here today and gone tomorrow. Life is short and transitory, a fact of which we are painfully aware. And so there must be some eternal truth, some unshakable promise on which to pin our hopes and our faith. We find this in God's Word, the Bible. This is the promise we find that starts to pull together some of the loose ends: ". . . [God] works out everything in conformity with the purpose of his will . . ." (Ephesians 1:11, NIV).

We also find a promise that we don't always understand but do believe. It's this: "We know that in all things God works for good with those who love him, those whom he has called according to his purpose" (Romans 8:28, TEV). Why did God take the one we love? We don't know, but we choose to believe that God does. We choose to believe that God knows what he's doing. We make a conscious choice to believe this, even if we don't always feel it.

There is nothing wrong with asking, "Why?" Ask it loud; ask it long. God is certainly able to cope with all our questions. You may find at least some of the answers. And if not the answers, at least some hints of the answers. If you find them, they probably will not be easy answers, but they will be *your* answers. There are no easy answers. And if you only keep coming up with questions, you can be certain that someday you will be able to find the answers. When

[3]Paraphrase of the *Heidelberg Catechism*.

we get to heaven, you can join us in the line. And it will be a long line.

Questions for Growth and Discussion

1. What are the right questions for you right now in your life?

2. How are you seeking answers to these questions?

3. What difficult questions would you like to ask God?

Today's date:_____

9

Under Reconstruction

You need to create a new identity. But you say, "But I don't want a new identity!" Perhaps not, but an essential part of the letting go process is to let go of the identity you had as your spouse's "other half." Letting go means that you accept the reality of your new situation. It doesn't mean that you deny the existence of the one you loved, or forget, or cut off the past. You *build* on the past because that past is a part of you. You build on the experiences of your past with the one you loved, on that relationship, and you grow and go on to become what you can become and what God intended for you to become.

To go through life acting as if your spouse were still alive, as if the marriage relationship still existed, or as if you are still the person you were before your loss is not to allow yourself to work through the grief process. It is essential that you develop a new identity. Herein lies both your greatest challenge and your greatest opportunity.

Your new identity doesn't spring up full-grown overnight! It grows gradually, slowly, painfully through the grieving process. Usually growth is only visible when you look back and say, "I was there and now I'm here. Look how far I've come!" Rather than denying the existence of the one you loved, your new identity simply recognizes the fact that the person *is* gone. Your new identity is built as new tasks are learned, new obstacles surmounted, new challenges met, new people found to help solve problems, new friends made, new enjoyments discovered, new opportunities found for service, new self-esteem discovered as you learn to do what you thought you couldn't do, and as you develop new vistas of hope and life.

Your New Identity

You face a number of choices in shaping a new identity.

"Who Am I?"

This is one of the right questions to be asking. Most people don't consciously choose their self-image or their life-style. Frequently career choices and marriage choices are made early in life. And the rest just sort of happens. So your self-image and life-style become molded by circumstances, by what everyone else says, instead of being chosen by you.

SELF-IMAGE AND LIFE-STYLE

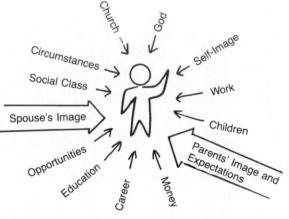

You have a unique opportunity that most people don't have. You have the opportunity to build a new self-image. You have the freedom to choose a life-style. Maybe you'll choose the same life-style that you've always had. Your self-image will have to change, but maybe it won't change much. Fine! But at least you will have come to a point at which *you* have the opportunity to choose. Maybe you will choose a different life-style or change your self-image, and that's OK, too. You didn't have any choice about losing your mate; you certainly wouldn't have made that choice. It was thrust on you. But now you *do* have the opportunity to choose. Whatever you choose is fine, as long as it's your choice!

This is *not* something you do early in your grief. Early in your grief, as much as possible, you want to keep things the way they are and not make any radical changes. But as you go through your grief, and grow through your grief, you come to the point where you are ready to evaluate your self-image and life-style and, if you so choose, make changes and alterations.

Establishing a New Self-Image and Life-Style

1. Come to these awarenesses:
   I'm a widowed person.
   I'm single.
   I'm OK.
   I'm a good person.
   God loves me and I do too.
   I have a future!

2. Ask these questions:
   What makes for happiness?
   What is important to me?
   What part of me is me and what's someone else?
   What do I want to do with my life?
   What were my dreams back then when I was alone?
   What is God saying to me?

3. All of this leads to:
   Introspection—belly-button gazing. (OK for a while as long as you don't get hung up there.)
   Testing of values. (Along with a lot of uneasiness.)
   Sampling of life-styles. (You may shock yourself!)
   Self-acceptance.
   Self-love.
   A new self-image.
   A life-style based on this new self-image.
   Positive goals for the future.

The Inner-Directed Life-Style

Many people's self-images have been determined by all these outside forces. You now have the opportunity to restructure your life-style from within. Who are you? What are you about? We've found it helpful to view life as a kind of wheel. There are various dimensions to life—mental, social, physical, and cultural/aesthetic. A well-balanced life needs all of these dimensions functioning in some kind of harmony. But for life to have meaning, at its center there must be a spiritual dimension. We see the spiritual dimension, your relationship with God, as being the hub of the new life-style you are building. Without the hub the wheel simply won't hold together. Life will not have meaning. So don't neglect your hub. Identify the ways in which you've grown spiritually through your grief process and make a plan for that growth to continue.

Decisions, Decisions

In the early phases of grief we urge you not to make any major decisions. Make only the decisions you have to make. Then make them wisely, using the best counsel available. People will try to rush you into making decisions too soon. Should I sell the house? Should I move to a retirement community in Florida? Should I go back to school, back to work, back to wherever? Take your time! Don't be pushed into making decisions. Grief takes a long, long time; you've got lots of time in which to decide. We urge you not to make any major decisions during the first year of your grief. But as you go— and grow—through the process, building self-confidence with each step along the way, you eventually come into the growth stage and are ready to start making decisions.

You still can take your time. You don't have to be hurried into making decisions. And you don't have to make any decisions that you don't want to make. You are in control of your life!

There are many people who will give you advice. You must weigh carefully to whom you will listen. Don't go only on your intuition. Many widowed persons have been taken in by people who seemed nice and honest. Beware! Don't listen to only one adviser. Even if Frank was your husband's financial adviser all these years, check around. Get other expert opinions. Never rely on just one expert. The wise advice of Scripture is, "In an abundance of counselors there is safety" (Proverbs 11:14b). This advice is repeated three times in Proverbs! (See also Proverbs 15:22 and 24:6.) So don't be timid about getting a second and third opinion, and then *you* decide!

What Does It Mean to Be Single?

It means about as many different things as there are single people. And today there are lots of single people! A great proportion of the adult population in our country today *is* single. So you're not alone. Some are widowed, many are divorced, and others have never married. Many resist the admission that they are single because of the stereotypes they have of what it means to be single. But we're all different people; so you can throw your stereotypes out the window!

You may not like it, but you *are* single. And the married life-style and the single life-style are different. You may not like it, you don't have to, but you need to accept it.

One of the most difficult aspects of your new single identity is your role as a sexual person. The intensity of this conflict will vary from person to person depending on many things. Widowed persons are not persons who have never married. They have known some degree of sexual fulfillment in their marriages; now they are alone. Too frequently we've offered easy answers without seriously grappling with the issues of postmarital sex. As we've said before, there are no easy answers in this area or in any other area.

You experience the loneliness and the longing for a companion of the opposite sex. It doesn't have to be physical! As one woman in our seminar said, "I'd just like the opportunity to hear a male voice and a male point of view once in a while."

You'd like Paula. She told us about attending an anniversary party for a couple she and her husband had known. As the evening progressed and the dancing began, she felt particularly alone and out of place. Quietly she slipped away to get her coat and leave. A physician whom she had known since high school followed her to the coatroom, helped her with her coat, and said, "You shouldn't be going out to your car alone." Paula said, "He put his arm around me and walked me to the car and kissed me on the cheek. It felt so good just to have an arm around me that I broke down in tears."

This is a difficult and confusing area in establishing a new lifestyle. Some of you are ready to move into dating, and others are not. Some will never wish to establish another relationship; others will. Some may find that their attitudes change. You may make some mistakes in this area. You may even do some things you'll later regret. But remember this is a learning process and a growth process.

Our society has blurred the distinction between the need for intimacy and the need for physical, sexual communication. What many formerly married people are looking for is intimacy, but what they often end up with is a sexual involvement which is premature, confusing, guilt-producing, and counterproductive. Many are looking only for the reassurance that they can still love and be loved. Widowed persons need to understand the difference between touching and intimacy. Coy Parsley has developed a "touching continuum" and an "intimacy continuum" which help us to distinguish between these two needs (see the chart that follows).[1] She encourages people to view both touching and intimacy as gifts that can be shared. What touching gifts and what intimacy gifts are you seeking? What gifts of touching and intimacy are you seeking to offer?

INTIMACY CONTINUUM	TOUCHING CONTINUUM
Watching	Seeing, hearing, smelling
Listening	Shaking hands
Chit-chatting	Greeting hug
Sharing ideas	Greeting kiss
Sharing personal backgrounds	Holding hands
Sharing deeper feelings	Sitting close and touching
Sharing secrets	Embracing
Profound friendship	Kissing
	Passionate kissing
	Necking
	Foreplay
	Sexual intercourse

Under Reconstruction

If there was a big sign over your life right now, it would probably read, "Under Reconstruction." Initially it feels more like "Under Demolition," but as you move through the grief process, you begin to feel that, rather than being demolished, your world is under reconstruction. Gradually as you move through your grief work and enter the growth phase, you begin to conceptualize a future. It is *your*

[1] Coy Parsley, "On Giving and Receiving Gifts," *Uplift*, X (March-April, 1978), p. 3.

future. Before, you might have had to take into account your spouse's plans, or you might have been dependent on your spouse's planning your future. But now *it's your future* and it's your responsibility. Make goals for your future. At first it may only be for the next week, or the next month, but gradually you'll come to the point where you can set long-range and even ambitious goals for your future.

You do have a future! It can be a good future if you are willing to set firm goals and work to make the goals become a reality. You've grown a long way and you've got a long way to grow!

If you knew that you couldn't fail, what would you want to do? That's a critical question. Many people don't try anything because they're afraid they might fail. But who wants to be a success at nothing? Who wants to come to the end of life and say, "Wow, I was a great success at nothing!" If you don't try, you'll never know. Sure, you'll never fail, but you'll never succeed either. And if you fail, so what? Who hasn't failed at some time in his or her life? You'll try again! But the chances of failure are lessened if you know what you want and have planned on how to get it.

That's where goals come in. A goal is nothing more than a statement of what you want. It needs to be written down very carefully so that you can be sure that you're saying *exactly* what you want. You'll find that once you make goals, you'll start achieving them. So be sure to write down exactly the goal you want. What? When? Where? Then sit down and figure how to get there. Do something like this:

Here's where I want to be.

Here's where I am.

Now how do I get from where I am to where I want to be? You write down the steps, as many as there are. Each step becomes an objective. You take the first step first. Remember: one step at a time. Inch by inch! Step by step! Take that step, then take the next, and the next, and the next, and you'll be surprised at how quickly you achieve your goals!

Caveat

"Let the reader beware!" If it's early in your grief, you may be thinking, "*What* are they talking about?" Where you are in your grief process will determine how helpful this chapter is to you now. If you've only recently suffered your loss, don't expect all this to make sense and be helpful. Your goal may only be to survive the next twenty-four hours. You cannot digest this book in one gulp! Come back later and reread this chapter again and again as you progress down the path of grief recovery. When you come back you'll find that because you've changed and grown, this chapter will read differently and you'll find a wealth of information that wasn't here before. This book is designed to be read and reread.

Questions for Growth and Discussion

1. Where are you in the process of building a new identity as a single person?

2. What are some of the parts of your self-image that came from your spouse that you don't want to lose?

3. If you knew you could not fail, what would *you* attempt to do?

4. List one goal that you've made for yourself for . . .
   Today:

   This week:

   This month:

   This year:

   Today's date:_____

10

How to Help Another Through Grief

We're aware that some of you at this moment aren't going through your own grief but are seeking a way to reach out and help another through grief. It may be a friend, a parent, or a neighbor. We're sure that reading this book has helped you in understanding the grief process and will better enable you to help your friend or loved one through his or her grief.

Many times you feel frustrated and helpless. Your friend has lost a loved one and is in pain. You want to help, you want to reach out in love, you want to do the right thing, but what is the best way to help? In this chapter we'll give you some specific suggestions as to how you can help.

Most of you are reading this book because your loved one has died. You are the one who is hurting. Now. But in the future it may be your friend or another loved one who is hurting, and you may be the one reaching out. Just going through the process yourself, although it certainly helps, doesn't guarantee that you will do the right thing in the right way.

Those who've experienced their own grief must always remind themselves that just as no two people are the same, no two grief experiences are the same. Don't be tempted to impress the mold of your grief experience on your grieving friend. Don't feel that because you've been through it you have all the answers—or any of the answers. But by now you should know what the questions are!

Don't be tempted to rehash your own grief so much that you don't allow your friend to share his or her feelings. It's fine to *share* feelings, but if you are primarily trying to help your friend, you'll do more listening than talking. Your experience will help, but you need to feel your way along sensitively, knowing when to share and when to listen. And you must always keep in mind that although there will

113

be many feelings with which you can identify, there may be some feelings and experiences which are uniquely a part of your friend's grief.

If your loved one has died and you're working through your own grief, you will find that it helps your own recovery process to reach out and share with another who is in need. Even if you aren't very far along the road to recovery, there is someone who's behind you on the path.

Recognize That Grief Is a Process and Takes Time

We live in a world of instant communication, instant tea, and fast food. We're impatient with anything that takes time, particularly a process which takes lots of time. "There must," we think, "be some way to speed it up!" That's the American way; only it doesn't work with grief. Research indicates that it may take from one to three years to work through the process of grief and that, even then, the changes brought about by a loss are so total, and so permanent, that one is always "growing" through his or her grief. We're all different, and each one of us goes through the grief process differently. Each person's grief process is unique. So don't push your friend. Never say, "OK, enough now! Come on, snap out of it!" Each grieving person must follow his or her own time schedule for recovery. You can best help by realizing this and by being patient.

Your friend is in the process of putting together a life which has been shattered. Visualize a banner over your friend's life reading, "Under Reconstruction." This rebuilding takes time; it simply cannot be rushed!

Be There

Dick says, "When I was a young pastor, just out of seminary, I used to worry about going to a home where there had just been a death. What would I say? What Bible passages would I read? What answers would I give? But over the years I've noticed that people who've lost a loved one don't care what I say or read. They won't remember because they're not hearing at the time. They are in shock. They just want me to be there. That's all—to be there. But being there can be so much!"

Really! Most people worry a great deal about what to say to the bereaved, but, especially during the first few weeks, nobody cares what you say. Your bereaved friend needs only to know that you're there. It's your presence that's important. When a loved one dies, there is such a gaping void that the mere presence of others is important. Presence doesn't fill the gap, but it does help one feel more secure. This is especially true after the funeral, after all the relatives and friends are gone. In the long month-to-month struggle that follows, that's when friends are most important.

Don't be afraid to reach out and touch somebody who is grieving. Sometimes a hug, a kiss on the cheek, or a handclasp says more than words could ever communicate!

Be careful that you don't take over. A person who is grieving is so wounded that it calls forth our protective instinct, and we want to shield and help the person by taking over and making decisions. Since the griever is numb with shock, he or she doesn't put up much resistance. It's nice to have people take over the routine household matters, but it is helpful for the griever to assume whatever responsibility he or she can. Be careful not to make decisions for the bereaved; instead, support him or her in making decisions. The grieving person feels his or her world has collapsed and he or she no longer has control. Allow the bereaved to feel some control, even if it's in small matters. Gradually, with encouragement, your friend can take control of more and more.

Allow Your Friend to Express Grief

Your friend is struggling to come to accept the fact that the person he or she loved is gone. Acceptance. Easy to say, but hard to do. You need to accept the fact that your friend is undergoing a profound reaction to loss called grief. Allow your friend to express his or her grief! Grief must be expressed! It can't be bottled up! Bottled-up grief is dangerous. Your friend will never come to any kind of acceptance and be able to move on until he or she has been allowed to express grief in some way. The person whom everyone admires and lauds with, "My, wasn't he strong and wonderful!" is being set up for problems. So don't encourage your friend to play a game of hide-and-seek, hiding his or her grief to seek your approval.

Listen Compassionately

Listening can be one of the best ways to help. We can't emphasize that enough! Let your friend talk about whatever he or she wants. If it is about the loved one, fine; listen. If the person doesn't want to talk about the deceased, don't push. Don't ask leading questions. Let him or her steer the conversation. Just listen. Most people want to talk too much rather than listen. We're uneasy, and so we try to cover our uneasiness by talking. Don't be afraid of long silences. Don't feel compelled to say something to break the silence. It will be hard, but if you bite your lip, you can keep silent. Don't think that in order to comfort, you have to be saying something. Many times your presence can mean much more than your words. Just listen!

Don't Give Easy Answers

There are no easy answers.

"It's God's will" is an easy answer if *you* give it. If your friend *arrives* at that conclusion, then it's not an easy answer. It's a difficult answer and it's the right one for him or her because it's *his* or *her* answer.

Many of us are too quick to start sermonizing or spouting Bible verses. There is a time for select Bible verses. There is great help and hope in the Bible for those who are bereaved. But usually the time when this help is most meaningful is further along in the grief process. It's best when the search for the right Bible verse is initiated by the griever.

C. S. Lewis wrote, "Talk to me about the truth of religion and I'll listen gladly. Talk to me about the duty of religion and I'll listen submissively. But don't come talking to me about the consolations of religion or I shall suspect that you don't understand."[1]

Joseph Bayly in *The Last Thing We Talk About* wrote:

> I was sitting, torn by grief. Someone came and talked to me of God's dealings, of why it happened, of hope beyond the grave. He talked constantly; he said things I knew were true.
> I was unmoved, except to wish he'd go away. He finally did.
> Another came and sat beside me. He didn't talk. He didn't ask leading questions. He just sat beside me for an hour and more, listened when I said something, answered briefly, prayed simply, left.
> I was moved. I was comforted. I hated to see him go.[2]

"Be thankful you were together for so long." "At least he didn't have to suffer." "At least his suffering is over." All easy answers. Sure, you're grateful for the years you had. And maybe he didn't suffer, or, if he did, you're glad he didn't suffer any more, but that doesn't lessen the loss.

Your friend isn't looking for answers—at least not from you—but for caring, compassionate friendship.

[1] C. S. Lewis, *A Grief Observed* (1966; reprint ed., Lawrence, Mass.: Merrimack Book Services, 1976), p. 28.

[2] Joseph Bayly, *The Last Thing We Talk About,* originally *The View from a Hearse* (Elgin, Ill.: David C. Cook Publishing Company, 1969, 1973), pp. 55-56.

Listen to and Accept Your Friend's Feelings

Whatever the feelings are, listen to them, and accept them. Feelings are not right or wrong; they *are*. And feelings need to be expressed—that's part of the way we work through feelings. Never say, "Now, now, you shouldn't feel that way." Your friend *does* feel that way! Feelings don't always make sense and that's OK too. Don't make judgments on your friend's feelings or try to rationalize them or explain them away; just listen.

Most of us want to be rational, logical. But grief isn't that way! It's fighting through a fog, a maze. It goes in one direction, then turns around and starts another way. It seems confusing to you as you watch your grieving friend laughing one moment, crying the next, then full of rage. But for healing and growth to occur, it's necessary to allow your friend to fight his or her way through this seemingly illogical process.

Some feelings, particularly strong feelings, make us uncomfortable. That's because many of us have been brought up to suppress our feelings and not express them. "Nice children don't feel that way." But feelings are! And part of the work of grief requires that feelings be expressed and discussed.

One particularly anxiety-producing moment comes when your friend says, "Sometimes I don't feel like going on. You know, I've sometimes felt like joining Margaret." Now before you hit the panic button, remember—feelings *are*. That your friend was willing to share this with you indicates a sense of trust. Listen! It is not unusual for grieving persons to think about suicide and feel, at least fleetingly, that it would deliver them from the pain that is so intense. You need to listen carefully to discover whether your friend is contemplating suicide as a possible alternative or is talking about how and when. In the helping profession, there is a general rule of thumb that you *always* take talk of suicide seriously. There is a popular, but dangerous, misconception that people who talk about suicide won't actually commit suicide. But that is false! So if you feel your friend is actually contemplating suicide, please get him or her professional help at once. Your friend's pastor or doctor is a good person to contact initially. If necessary, volunteer to go with your friend to the first appointment.

Don't Be Afraid of Tears

Crying is normal, an expected, essential part of expressing grief. Many times people feel they're helping if they can keep the grieving person from crying. So they encourage people to contain their grief and not express it in tears. We once did a seminar for a funeral home, and the main concern of the funeral director was what would happen if the people in the seminar started crying. He wanted to be sure that we'd be able to get them stopped! We just asked him to have lots of tissues handy.

Many of us are afraid of tears. We're afraid that another's tears might start us crying; we somehow perceive this as a sign of weakness. But crying is a God-given way of relieving, releasing, and cleansing. You need to communicate to your friend, not necessarily verbally but at least by your attitude, "It's OK to cry. It's part of your healing, and I understand." The goal isn't to push your friend to get weepy but to recognize that there are happy memories and sad memories; sometimes they both bring tears and that's OK.

Often the most significant thing that Dick has done, when as a pastor he's gone to a home where there's just been a death, is to sit and be with the family and cry with them. Dick says, "I've never yet had a family say, 'Thank you for what you said when you came over.' But I've had them say, 'I'll never forget that you came over that night, and sat there at the kitchen table with us, and cried with us.'" As a friend you care and you want to share. Reach out and don't worry about yourself or your tears.

Be sensitive to the mood of the bereaved. Sometimes they want to talk and sometimes they want to be silent. Sometimes they want to cry and sometimes they want to laugh.

Don't Deny the Existence of the Deceased

There! I just did! Don't refer to the "deceased" but to Harry or Mildred. The person who has died had a name and an identity. He or she built a relationship with your friend. Because the person is gone doesn't mean the feelings of the relationship have ended. When you carefully excise the name of Mildred and Harry from conversation, refuse to talk about them, and avoid the remembrance of happy times you shared together, you are denying their existence. Rob said, "The hardest thing about my wife's death is that no one talks about her anymore."

Nikki's father died not long ago. Her mother has a friend she frequently sees who will say, "Harland was such an inspiration to me. I never would have had the courage to teach Sunday school if he hadn't helped me." Or, "Remember the time our dog walked into the church while Harland was preaching?" She isn't afraid to share memories, and, more importantly, she isn't afraid to say that Nikki's dad's life meant something to her and to others. He wasn't blotted out of existence. He meant something . . . and he still does.

When you advise, "Forget the past. Live for today and tomorrow!" you are denying the existence of the person who has died. Yes, life does go on. Slowly some of the ties of the relationship are released, and some of the emptiness is filled in other ways. But because two lives have touched, the person who remains is never quite the same. The person who has died is eternally a part of your friend, and tucked away will always be the memory of and love for that special person.

Accept Your Own Mortality

Many of us have difficulty relating to grieving friends because we have not been able to come to grips with our own mortality and the mortality of people we love. Unable to accept the prospect of our own death or the death of our family members, we are unable to reach out to those who have lost loved ones.

While it is possible in this life to cultivate a relationship with God that will prepare us for the next life, it is an inescapable fact that we will all die. Sometimes in order to face life, we have to accept the reality of death. Sometimes in order to reach out and help another through grief, we have to contemplate the death of our loved ones and our grief as well as our death and the grief of those who love us.

That's not easy. It can be painful, and it's a price not everyone is willing to pay. But if we can "walk through" the valley of our own grief and mortality we will come out on the other side more aware, more alive, more grateful, and more able to reach out and help another.

Take the Initiative

At the funeral the bereaved is inundated by offers of help. Some people offer to help because they don't know what else to say, and others really do want to help. "Now, really, Mary, let me know if there is anything I can do." You wait. Perhaps Mary never asks you to do anything; so you don't. But what you don't realize is that Mary desperately needs to feel in control. She doesn't want to be a burden to anyone or impose. Frightened as she is, dismal as her situation may be, Mary feels she needs to start coping. So she doesn't ask, although she could certainly use your help and friendship during this time. So take the initiative! Without walking all over Mary, you might call up and say, "Mary, how about letting me take your car in to get it ready for winter?" Or, "Say, let's go over and look at the antique show at the mall and grab a sandwich for lunch."

If you want to help, there's plenty you can do. Some things you can do immediately. Other things you can do three weeks, six months, a year later. But you take the initiative!

Find a Need and Fill It

Offer to handle the telephone, notifying relatives and friends and taking incoming calls. After someone has died, everyone wants to call and express sympathy and love, but there are times when the bereaved is too drained to take another call.

Help with out-of-town guests. Offer your guest room. Help with transportation, picking people up at the airport and getting people to and from the funeral home. Lend the family your extra car. Offer to baby-sit for children. Help clean the house and keep it clean. (You need to be careful here—check first so that you don't disrupt anything that may contain a memory of the person who has died. The garage may be a mess, but maybe that was the last thing Jim was working on before he died. Be sensitive!)

Bring food. Not everyone feels like eating, but many times there are out-of-town guests who do need to eat. We'll never forget when Nikki's dad died how the neighbors organized to keep us fed. Unobtrusively at mealtimes food appeared; we'd eat, and the dishes were wisked away like magic! It was one area we didn't have to think about or worry about. It just happened—thanks to a lot of caring neighbors!

What About Flowers?

We love flowers and enjoy them, but we're not much for flowers at funerals. It always seems to be such a waste. We buy flowers now so that we can enjoy them! Even if the family doesn't specify "No flowers," we'd suggest that you express your sympathy and love in a way that reflects better stewardship. Most families want to give flowers for the casket, and that's really the only floral piece they're concerned about. When Nikki's dad died, we placed a simple but beautiful bundle of wheat on the casket. It reminded us of Jesus' promise of resurrection: "Unless a grain of wheat falls into the earth and dies, it remains alone; but if it dies, it bears much fruit. He who loves his life loses it, and he who hates his life in this world will keep it for eternal life" (John 12:24-25).

If not flowers, then what? Most families would rather have you make a donation to their church than send a big display of flowers that they won't see or be able to enjoy. Almost every church sets up a memorial fund to honor and express thanksgiving for the life of the one who has died. The church acknowledges your gift not only to you but also to the family, although normally it acknowledges only the receipt of your gift and not the amount.

Flowers *are* meaningful after the funeral. No big spread of flowers but, several weeks or a month after, a small planter, a little bouquet, or a single rose. Add a note saying something like, "I love you and am thinking of you!" That will mean more than you'll ever know, certainly more than a mountain of withering flowers at the cemetery

Flowers can be appropriate even much later. And they may help your friend through anniversary times, which can be particularly difficult. Virginia told us how she'd never forget the friends who sent her, on the first anniversary of her husband's death, a single rose with a card that read, "Frank was such a wonderful man! We miss him too. We love you and are thinking of you and praying for you today." What a treasure to have friends like that!

Call Up and Just Say, "Hi!"

There are always lots of people around until the funeral. Then they all leave. The out-of-town company goes home, and the house is alone and empty. Then begins the long, lonely process of working through grief. Those who really want to help take the initiative. Pick up the phone and call. What will you say? Start by saying, "Hi!" If your friend doesn't feel like talking, fine. Call again next week.

How About Dinner?

Don't wait for your friend to call you, you take the initiative. Have lunch! Have brunch. Even breakfast at McDonald's. It doesn't have to be a big deal. You're not going for the food but for the friendship! Invite your friend over for dinner. But wait! You can invite just your friend. It *is* possible for a person to eat and enjoy a meal as a single. Don't feel that you have to invite all the widows and widowers in your church to join you. Don't feel you have to invite the distinguished widower who works in your husband's office to join you. Just invite your friend. Yes, Harry won't be there as he always was in the past.

Harry is dead. But your friend isn't, and why can't she still continue to be your friend?

The most common complaint we hear from widows, particularly, is that they feel excluded after their husbands die. They feel cut off from people who'd always been their mutual friends. Frequently husbands will say to their wives, "Oh, you ask Mabel to lunch or a night out with you. You women can relate better." But we hear widows saying how much they miss a male voice, or a male perspective, and how wonderful it is to have a *couple* take a widow out.

And, yes, you can talk about Harry! The time you all went camping and Harry tripped over the tent rope and the whole tent collapsed. Some tears may drip into the beef bourguignon, but they will add just the right touch of saltiness, and love!

A word of caution about the terms "widow" and "widower." We've used them in this book because they help describe the grieving persons that much of this book is about. But the terms *can be* very annoying. Some people do *not* want to be described as "widows" or "widowers." One woman emphatically put it, "I'm not a widow; I'm Pat!" Find out what your friend thinks about the term before using it. Ask again a few months later. You'll find that feelings often change.

Here I Am!

Don't wait for an invitation; just drop in. Grieving persons are going through a multitude of struggles. No matter how great your friendship, they realize a change has taken place that affects all areas of their lives, and they are afraid to impose. You take the initiative. "Hi, Mary, thought I'd come over and rake up the leaves and put the lawnmower away for the winter. I know Paul always used to do that." You'll be a godsend! For Mary those leaves tower higher than the World Trade Center, and she's never put a lawnmower away for the winter in her life!

There are many things you can do to help! Every widow has a dozen little chores that need to be done around the house that would be on her husband's Saturday R & R ("repair and renovate") list if he were still alive. And almost every widower would love a home-cooked meal that he didn't have to make. Or perhaps a treat, a recipe you got from his wife, maybe her specialty. When you make it, it won't taste quite the same, but the thought will definitely be there.

Still, Still Be There

Months and years after, the bereaved person still needs someone to listen. Even if you've heard the story a hundred times before, if you're a real friend who wants to help, you'll listen for the hundred-and-first time.

Don't be intimidated by what you hear. Don't judge. Maybe your friends weren't as happily married as you thought. A good friend can listen, listen, listen, and not repeat.

Share This Book!

If this book has opened new vistas of understanding, why not share it with a friend? Don't give him or her your copy; buy one as a gift (of course!). We hope you will want to keep this book handy. You'll need to read and reread it. As you move along the path of grief recovery and reread it, there are sections that will be meaningful to you that perhaps you cannot relate to now. As you grow, this book will help you in new and different ways.

If you bought this book primarily to help someone else through his or her grief, keep your copy for the time when the grief is not your friend's but your own. That time will come.

This is, after all, your book. As you've read it, we hope you've marked it up—the only way to read a book!—underlining passages, starring those sections that particularly apply to you, and dog-earing pages you want to refer to again. We hope you've interacted with us, writing your own personal responses to the growth and discussion questions in order to make this your *personal* book.

If this book has helped you, it will probably help your friend. Your friend may not read it right away, but he or she will read it when ready. Get your friend a copy to have when it is needed. The pain of grief is so great and the anxiety of not understanding what's happening is so severe that we wish every grieving person could have a copy of this book handy. We can't take away the pain, but we can help to make it more understandable and thus lessen the anxiety.

Questions for Growth and Discussion

For Those Trying to Recover from Grief

1. What was the most thoughtful, helpful thing that someone did for you? Could you do this, or something similar, for someone else?

2. What are the resources that you've found in your community? For future reference, list the names and phone numbers here.

For Those Who Are Trying to Reach Out and Help

1. So nobody's perfect! What are some of the things that perhaps you would do differently or say differently if you could do them over?

2. What are three specific ways that you could offer to help your friend through this time?

3. What does your friend say to you that makes you uneasy? Why does it make you uneasy? For the sake of your friend can you work through your own feelings?

Today's date:_____